Employment Security

Employment Security

BALANCING HUMAN AND ECONOMIC CONSIDERATIONS

PAUL H. LOSEBY

QUORUM BOOKS

WESTPORT, CONNECTICUT • LONDON

Library of Congress Cataloging-in-Publication Data

Loseby, Paul H.
    Employment security : balancing human and economic considerations
/ Paul H. Loseby.
      p.   cm.
    Includes bibliographical references and index.
    ISBN 0-89930-692-6 (alk. paper)
    1. Job security—United States.   I. Title.
HD5708.45.U6L67   1992
331.25'96—dc20   92-1132

British Library Cataloguing in Publication Data is available.

Library of Congress Catalog Card Number: 92-1132
ISBN: 0-89930-692-6

First published in 1992

Quorum Books, 88 Post Road West, Westport, CT 06881
An imprint of Greenwood Publishing Group, Inc.

Printed in the United States of America

The paper used in this book complies with the
Permanent Paper Standard issued by the National
Information Standards Organization (Z39.48-1984).

10 9 8 7 6 5 4 3 2 1

Contents

Illustrations

TABLES

FIGURES

1
Introduction

Throughout the 1980's large-scale layoffs of employees by American companies were commonplace. The layoffs were not confined to industrial workers; clerical, technical, professional, and managerial employees were also released in large numbers. The recession of 1990-1991 produced similar impacts on both industrial and white-collar employees. Although called a "white-collar" recession, numbers published in 1991 showed a different story. In June 1991 unemployment among managers and professionals stood at 2.8 percent, up from 2.2 percent a year earlier. But the jobless rate for skilled blue-collar workers had jumped to 7.8 percent from 5.2 percent. And for workers with no technical skills, the rate rose to 11.5 percent from 8.5 percent.[1] "It is true that this (1990–1991) has been a broad based recession, and that no industry except maybe health services has escaped it. But it's pretty clear that the hardest hit are the blue collar workers," said Phil Rones, senior economist at the Federal Bureau of Labor Statistics.

Though the numbers show the blue-collar jobs to be hardest hit, the professional positions continue to receive much attention in the media. Projections for future opportunities in white-collar jobs will continue to challenge the job market. Salaried professionals who work as part of a bureaucracy rather than in private practice have proven to be particularly vulnerable to layoff. First of all, they are not typically in decision-making positions where they can fight for their jobs. Second, most professionals are non-union and have often been accused of having as much allegiance to their profession and professional society as they do to their employer. Hence, when layoffs do occur, it may be relatively easy to dismiss a presumably uncommitted professional employee regardless of that individual's technical contribution to the firm.[2]

PUBLIC SECTOR

Public sector employees are also finding their jobs in jeopardy in a number of states, and with the federal government. Although the absolute numbers of public employees in the federal sector, and in state and local government (including education), continues to climb, the rate of growth of public sector jobs is declining significantly. This is said to be the result of the so-called taxpayers' revolt against inflation and public spending that has affected all levels of government. This has resulted in hiring freezes and staff cutbacks in many public agencies, much the same as in the private sector.

In the past, public employees have traditionally enjoyed a significantly higher level of employment security than the private sector. This was generally accepted and deemed to be equitable by many as a trade-off because of lower salaries typically paid. The gap between wages and salaries has narrowed considerably, and, while civil service and tenure laws still insulate many public employees from the direct consequences of the fluctuating economy, that protection does not appear as strong as it once was.[3]

Some laws protecting employment for public employees are under scrutiny by "new style" legislative proposals, which include state and federal bills introduced to abolish tenure and substantially modify the existing civil service system.[4]

PRIVATE SECTOR

A survey of 1,005 corporations conducted jointly by Fortune and the Wyatt Company consulting firm has found that 86 percent of the companies have reduced their managerial ranks in the past five years, 52 percent of them in 1990. Managerial downsizing has taken even deeper hold in companies with more than 5,000 employees. Ninety percent of these firms have slashed the number of employees in white-collar positions over the past five years; 59 percent in 1990. Probably even more noteworthy, 41 percent of the top human resource executives polled say that the ranks of managers are likely to shrink in the next five years. Only 25 percent expect the number to grow.[5]

Among reasons for dismissals in the private sector were economic recession, technological change (causing skill-match challenges), competitive pressures (including those stemming from foreign competition and from deregulation of previously regulated industries), mergers and corporate restructuring, and the belief that the best staff is a lean staff. Employee layoffs are by no means a recent phenomenon. They have long been used by American companies to adjust to declines in their economic fortunes. Reduction in staff through layoff has been accepted by U.S. businesses as a quick way to rid themselves of surplus

employees, reduce costs, raise productivity, and increase profitability.

COSTS OF UNEMPLOYMENT

Unemployment is costly to many segments of society, yet
many of those costs are hidden. There are economic and human
costs, with considerable overlap between categories, and one
category of cost often affects another.

One of the biggest losses caused by unemployment is lost
output. This includes unused plant output, houses that are not
built, urban transit systems that are not produced, social and
health care workers who are not hired, and so on. The magnitude
of this loss is not trivial. The 1975 recession, during which the
jobless rate rose from 5.6 percent in 1974 to 8.5 percent in 1976,
was estimated by the Senate Budget Committee to have cost the
nation $200 billion in lost production—nearly $1,000 for every
man, woman, and child.[6]

A study published in 1977 by the University of California
economist Steven Sheffrin showed that unemployment significantly reduces the living standards of many Americans. Sheffrin
measured the cumulative costs of continued employment from
1956 to 1976. His basic assumption used to analyze the costs of
unemployment assumed that employment had been maintained
at 4.1 percent. This is the rate that existed in 1956, a peacetime
year during the Eisenhower administration. His calculations
show that failure of the U.S. economy to maintain that rate of
unemployment cost the nation $2.3 trillion (in 1976 dollars) in
lost production over that twenty-year period. This loss was
estimated to be the equivalent of 17 percent of the 1976 total
production of goods and services—Gross National Product—in
the United States.[7] To pursue this further, if U.S. unemploy-

ment had been reduced from the 4.1 percent range in 1956 to a common European range of 2 percent, the additional GNP in 1976 alone, according to Sheffrin's estimate, would have generated $100 billion in additional tax revenues.[8] This additional $100 billion could have financed all of the following:

- raised the entire poor population up to the government official poverty line income at an estimated cost of $16 billion,
- established a national health insurance program for an additional $64 billion, and
- increased public anti-pollution expenditures by another $18 billion per year to clean up the environment by the mid-1980's.

Although these are speculations and deal with the financial side of the equation, unemployment has also taken its toll on the human side of the equation. A major study, completed in 1976 by M. Harvey Brenner of Johns Hopkins University for the Joint Economic Committee of Congress, evaluated the social and human impact of unemployment.

Brenner found that a sustained one-percentage-point increase in the unemployment rate in the United States was associated five years later with a:

- 1.9 percent increase in total mortality and mortality from cardiovascular-renal disease and from cirrhosis of the liver
- 4.1 percent increase in suicides
- 3.4 percent increase in state mental hospital admissions and
- 5.7 percent increase in homicide.[9]

Although the percentages are a small proportion of total numbers, when translated into human terms Brenner calculated that a one-percentage-point increase in the jobless rate is associated with 36,887 total deaths, including 20,240 deaths from cardiovascular-renal causes; 920 suicides; 648 homicides; 495 deaths from cirrhosis of the liver; 4,227 admissions to state mental hospitals; and 3,340 additional admissions to state prison systems.[10]

The question seems to come down to "what is an acceptable and affordable (from financial and human aspects) level of unemployment?" that should be targeted. Also, what are the various controllable causes? Are American businesses, government and other interested stakeholders willing to address and give top priority to the issue so that layoffs can be reduced to a more acceptable number. A question that arises asks, "can we guarantee lifetime employment?" What does the guarantee really mean, who is covered, and how? One must start with a definition of what is expected and what is meant by *guaranteed employment*, or employment security, as offered by some companies.

RISKS WITH EMPLOYMENT SECURITY

Employment security is viewed by some executive managers as very risky to a firm's profitability and longevity. For example, Alexander B. Trowbridge, president of the National Association of Manufacturing, views employment security as negative and terms it "very dangerous". "Guaranteed jobs can mean enormous costs, reduced flexibility in management and investment decisions, and reduced funds available for technological modifications to increase productivity," said Trowbridge, a former president of the Conference Board.

Edward L. Cushman, former American Motors vice president for labor relations, agrees, says the Bureau of National

Affairs. "The hard cold fact in an economy changing so rapidly," Cushman says, is that "job security is dependent on the employer's competitive ability and on economic forces beyond the employer's control."

Economist Thomas Kochan, a professor at the Massachusetts Institute of Technology, is quoted as saying that job guarantees would be particularly risky "on the down side," with the costs likely to get out of hand during a major recession.[11]

As noted, the risks are sizable for an enterprise because of cyclical economic change, limited control over governmental fiscal policy, global competition, and market instability. Some companies provide employment security at various levels, and commit to protect jobs for their employees within reason. This commitment, although often not ironclad, is sufficient to gain employee loyalty, commitment, and flexibility.

EMPLOYMENT SECURITY DEFINED

When lifetime employment is mentioned, the Japanese image often comes to mind as a result of stories and examples that proliferate in the press. The Japanese guarantee is less of a model than it appears. "Japanese lifetime employment" covers, according to most estimates, just 15 to 35 percent of the workforce, and applies almost exclusively to males working for big firms. Furthermore, it is maintained through a series of strong-arm tactics such as:

1. pulling in subcontract work, on short notice from small firms,
2. using women in temporary, unprotected roles to absorb peak demand, and
3. massive redeployment of people to sales in troubled times.

The word *guarantee* is an ambiguous and general term used by some United States companies in describing their employment security practice. There are few guarantees in the United States that are provided to employees in writing, except for union contracts. Most are oral agreements that profess to protect employees' jobs at all reasonable costs, and guard against layoffs. These agreements in many cases are explicitly demonstrated through decades of practicing no layoffs. Even the Lincoln Electric Company written guarantee, which has been successful in protecting the jobs of its employees for over fifty consecutive years, is not hard and fast; it can be changed, with six months' advance notice, by a vote of the firm's board of directors.

Tom Peters, in his book *Thriving on Chaos*, provides a listing of variables often used to determine whose employment is guaranteed, along with some definitions. These indicate the variety that is present in the economy and include:

1. Different classes of employees may enjoy different degrees of employment security. For example, managers normally have greater security than blue-collar employees.
2. Permanent employees have more employment security than temporary employees.
3. Length of service may determine the degree of security.
4. Certain changes, but not others, may be covered. For example, employees may be secure against technological changes, but not against plant closures.
5. Occupation and wages may be altered. Employees may be assured of permanent employment, but not necessarily in the current position or occupation or at the current wage level, and not necessarily with the current employer.
6. Employment may be offered in a different location. For example, a displaced employee may be transferred to a different job in the same community by outplacement to a different employer.

7. Certain aspects of employment may be protected and not others, such as weekly earnings, an hourly rate, a minimum number of working hours per year, and so on. Thus the job is protected, but the terms of employment are modified temporarily.

8. Security may be contingent on acceptance of certain conditions, such as mandatory overtime, internal transfer at management's discretion, and blurring of jurisdictional lines.

9. Negotiated concessions may be required, such as wage reductions, benefit modifications, and work-rule relaxations.

10. Security may apply for a limited period of time (such as for the duration of a collective agreement), or for the work life of the employee (as in the case of the newspaper typographers, longshoremen, and others).[12]

Peters writes that "the more restrictive the definition of *guarantee*, the less trust is engendered and the less the benefit to the firm." His recommendation is for a broad definition, accompanied by strategies and tactics that allow the firm to live up to its promise.

As shown, a number of definitions and interpretations of employment security are offered by writers on the subject and firms that practice it. The one definition that best describes the subject and intent as used in this context is simply stated: *Employment (job) security is a practice that protects full-time workers against the loss of employment and earnings for reasons unrelated to their job performance or behavior.*

The definition is not meant to imply that a specific job to which a person is assigned will be protected for a period of time, but rather that there will be a job, at some capacity, for that person within the organization if the present job is eliminated for any reason. The employer has the responsibility to balance work and move people to jobs (or jobs to people), and the employee has the responsibility to perform the assigned work in a satisfactory manner.

HISTORICAL PERSPECTIVE

Karl Marx, writing in the 19th century, considered depressions (recessions) and unemployment inevitable under capitalism. The business cycle, with its alternating periods of contraction and expansion, has been proven to be the norm under the terminology entitled capitalist development. Marx viewed the unemployed as an "industrial reserve army vital to the functioning of the capitalist system." As a readily available supply of labor, the unemployed feed the system in times of economic expansion. Unemployment was also seen by Marx as a way to help increase a company's profitability by restraining the wages of employed workers, who could always be replaced by unemployed. To Marx and his followers, "capitalism without unemployment was as unattainable as socialism with unemployment."[13]

More than 100 years have passed since labor in the United States began the struggle to achieve an eight-hour workday, down from the twelve- to fourteen-hour day that was normal at that time. The shortened days were an attempt by management to distribute work that was becoming scarce in the wake of mechanization and improved technologies. Periodic unemployment was a problem in those early days of industrialization, just as employment security is a problem for workers in today's economy. Layoffs in the automobile, steel, rubber, textile, and electronics industries over the last few years attest to the problem of employment insecurity and changing job-skill requirements of jobs within U.S. corporations.

Although employment security has never been universally pursued in the United States, it has been in existence worldwide for many years. One early example took place in 1806 in a cotton mill owned by Robert Owen in New Lanmark, Scotland. The mill was faced with an abrupt reduction in the supply of raw materials caused by an American embargo. Most of the other millers shut down operations and fired their workers. Owen was forced to stop the machinery, but kept paying full wages and assigned people to maintenance tasks during the four-month crisis. Owen reaped the reward as his workforce was subsequently more amenable to managerial, organizational, and technological changes. The workers supported constant innovation that led to extraordinary long-term profitability relative to competitors.[14] Some 150 years later, employment security continues to attract attention, but with limited interest from business executives. Fewer than five percent of the *Fortune* 500 industrial companies subscribed to the practice in the mid-1980's (Table 1.1). Some companies listed have since discontinued the practice of employment security and others are no longer in existence.

The reasons for this reluctance are varied, yet discernable. The generally accepted practice of U.S. companies in handling unexpected declines in workload continues to be through the use of employee layoff.

PRACTICING COMPANIES

Some U.S. companies view workload fluctuations differently and practice employment security during favorable and unfavorable times. Fel-Pro, IBM, and Bank of America are three examples of such companies, which have each continued

Table 1.1:

U.S. Organizations Practicing Employment Security (published sources from the mid-1980s)

Advanced Micro Devices*
Avon Products*
Bank of America
Bell Laboratories
Boeing Corporation*
Chaparral Steel
Control Data*
Dana Corporation*
Data General*
Delta Airlines
Digital Equipment Corporation*
E. I. Du Pont de Nemours*
Eli Lilly*
Exxon Corporation*
Federal Express
Fel-Pro
Fort Howard Paper*
Gordon-Rupp
Hallmark Cards, Inc.
Herman Miller*
Hewitt Associates
Hewlett-Packard*
H. P. Hood
International Business Machines*

LGA
Levi Strauss
Lincoln Electric Company
Mallinckrodt
Manufacturers Hanover
Materials Research Corp.
Minnesota Mining (3M)*
Morgan Guaranty
Motorola*
Nissan U.S.
Nucor Steel Corporation*
Olga Company
People Express Airline
Piggly Wiggly Carolina
Pitney Bowes*
Provincetown-Boston Air
Quill Corporation
R. J. Reynolds Tobacco Co.*
S. C. Johnson
Tandem Computers*
Tektronix*
Tennant
Upjohn*
Worthington Industries*
Wyeth Laboratories

* *Fortune* 500 Companies, 25 April 1988, D11-D30.

Data sources:
Across The Board, January 1985, 37.
Harvard Business Review, July–August 1985, 32.
Employment Security in a Free Economy, 1984, 19.

the practice for more than 50 years. It has been predicted by some that the wave of the future will follow the example of these three. It has been suggested by a number of management practitioners and academic theorists that the cost of layoff can be excessive, disruptive to the organization, and negatively effect employee productivity.[15]

The challenge, however, will be to convince the majority that such a practice is financially feasible and practical in serving the employee, the company, and society.

RECENT DROPOUTS

The survival of employment security among the U.S. *Fortune* 500 industrial corporations is questionable at best. The number of companies that initiate a job security practice after being in business for a number of years are few. In recent years a number of companies that had maintained a strong commitment to the practice have modified their thinking to address economic survival.

Data from a recent study verify the difficulty in sustaining employment security through cyclical times, mergers, acquisitions, and internal corporate restructuring. In 1947 the office of War Mobilization and Reconversion compiled a list of 196 U.S. firms practicing employment security.[16] Thirty years later Audrey Freedman, senior research associate with *The Conference Board*, found that only one of those plans—Hormel's—was still in existence, and today it too is gone.

Further research has shown that in most cases employment security no longer existed due to the fact that the business disappeared. Each of the businesses has a different story and not all failed. For example, Procter and Gamble and Quaker Oats were listed as employment-secure companies in 1947 but mergers and sale of divisions prompted their actions causing removal from the list. It should also be noted that even those surviving firms listed in the late 1970's did not necessarily exist in their earlier form.[17]

An example of a more recent change by a major corporation is Eastman Kodak, which discontinued its practice in the late 1970's. This departure from employment security was decided after company sales became sluggish following many years of domination in its industry. Other major corporations that have discontinued employment security in recent years include Intel, Texas Instruments, Data General, American Telephone and Telegraph, Advanced Micro Devices, and most recently, in the early months of 1991, Digital Equipment Corporation (DEC).

ADVANTAGES AND DISADVANTAGES

The practice of employment security is resisted by management in the United States for a number of reasons. Many of these are based on perception that disadvantages outweigh advantages, with labor costs given as one of the primary reasons for the wave of layoffs in the manufacturing sector. Is has been suggested that these costs might better be contained and controlled in other ways. In a survey of manufacturers completed by the National Association of Accountants it was determined that on the average, labor costs represent only 15 percent of the total cost of making a product. Based on this data is was suggested that rather than layoff, successful cost reduction programs might be studied. This would uncover areas where freed-up energy from doing unneeded work could be spent on increasing revenues and boosting profits, according to John Neumann, a consultant with Management Practice. Says Neumann: "There's a very long list of things you can do without firing people. Most companies do only one or two and then run early retirement (programs)."[18] Companies that have been successful in doing what Neumann has suggested are Lincoln Electric and IBM—both have redeployed surplus people to sales or customer support during cyclical downturns.

Some disadvantages of employment security that are often noted by human resource and business executives include the following:

- employment security is expensive when a company experiences unexpected workload declines and/or change in required job skills,
- workload and manpower requirements are difficult to predict because of rapid technological change,
- mergers and acquisitions introduce another level of complexity to workload planning, and
- employment security greatly reduces company flexibility to react to fluctuating economic conditions within the national and global marketplaces.

This list is not all-inclusive, but rather presents insight into real and perceived challenges of predicting workload requirements within the uncertain and dynamic environment of human resource planning.

Advantages of employment security are based largely on perception, with few statistical studies to support beliefs. Some advantages and beliefs addressed by this same group of human resource and business level executives include:

- improved employee loyalty based on reduced fear of job loss,
- reduced expense and improved quality as a result of lower employee turnover,

Table 1.2

Costs and Benefits of Employment Security

Costs:

Extra payroll and payroll-related expenses:
- training costs
- temporary red-circle rates
- extra overtime due to reluctance to hire
- extra costs of any special early retirement programs

Moving expenses

Possible slower delivery schedule

Productivity losses associated with people assigned to different jobs

Extra financial charges because of larger than necessary inventory

Extra employment costs associated with extreme selectivity in hiring

Possible slower rate of methods or technological change due to need to avoid displacing permanent employees

Benefits:

Better employee morale because of lack of job insecurity

Productivity advantages associated with less employee resistance to methods, or to technological changes due to fear of job loss

Greater acceptance of methods and technological change

Lower unemployment insurance costs

Savings of subsequent employment and training if there had been a layoff

Favorable image in the community

Source: *Personnel Policies in Large Non-Union Companies*, 1980, 118.

- increased employee productivity, and
- improved employee morale.

The debate encompassing and comparing the balance between advantages and disadvantages continues. It provokes thought in the minds of scholars, and raises the curiosity of business executives whose concern is survival for the national, and often global, corporations that they are charged with managing. A list that compares anticipated costs of employment security with expected benefits can be seen in Table 1.2. Each study or analysis undertaken to learn the effects of employment security has merit. This work effort is an attempt to clarify some of the issues, or at a minimum increase the platform of cognizance for the timely topic of employment security.

Ramifications of providing employment security will be addressed to include employee and management views. Discussion will center around social, financial, and human resource implications as viewed by writers and company stakeholders (customers, financial institutions, stockholders, etc.). This effort will attempt to clarify findings of recent studies on the subject, with a focus on substantiating claims made by critics and proponents of employment security.

NOTES

1. Mary Kane, "White Collar Recession Has Changed Color," *The Times*, Trenton N.J., 21 July 1991, D1.

2. Joseph A. Raelin, "Job Security for Professionals," *Personnel*, July 1987, 40.

3. Robert E. Doherty, Director, Institute of Public Employment, New York State School of Industrial and Labor Relations, Cornell University.

4. June Weisberger, *Job Security & Public Employees*, (Ithaca, N.Y.: New York State School of Industrial and Labor Relations, Cornell University, 1973), 9.

5. Dave Kirkpatrick, "The New Executive—Unemployed," *Fortune*, 8 April 1991, 37.

6. U.S. Senate Committee on the Budget, First Concurrent Resolution on the Budget—Fiscal Year 1976, Report that Accompanied S. Con. Res. 32, 94th Congress 1st Session, 1975, 5.

7. Steven Sheffrin, "The Costs of Unemployment," with an introduction by Gar Alperovitz and Jeff Faux (Washington, D.C.: Exploratory Project for Economic Alternatives, 1977).

8. Ibid., 9–13.

9. M. Harvey Brenner, "Estimating the Costs of National Economic Policy: Implications for Mental and Physical Health and Aggression," Study Prepared for the Joint Economic Committee, U.S. Congress, 94th Congress, 2nd Session, 1976, VI.

10. Ibid., 5.

11. Jerome M. Rosow and Robert Zager, "The Case for Employment Security," *Across the Board*, January 1985, 36.

12. Tom Peters, *Thriving on Chaos* (New York: Harper & Row, Publishers, 1988), 417–418.

13. Helen Ginsberg, *Full Employment and Public Policy: The United States and Sweden* (Lexington, Mass.: Lexington Books D. C. Heath and Company, 1983), 7–8.

14. Ibid., 414–415.

15. Gary B. Hansen, "Preventing Layoffs: Developing an Effective Job Security and Economic Adjustment Program", *U.S. Department of Labor BLMR 102*, Bureau of Labor Management Relations and Cooperative Programs, Washington, D.C., 1986, 1.

16. Audrey Freedman, "Security Bargains Reconsidered," New York: The Conference Board, 1978.

17. Diane Riggan, "Employment Security Revisited in the '80s," *Personnel Administrator*, December 1985, 71.

18. Bill Saporito, "Cutting Costs Without Cutting People," *Fortune*, 25 May 1987, 27.

2
External Influences

American industry has experienced a number of major changes in the recent past that sets the stage for the future: the slowdown of U.S. inflation, the fall in the value of the dollar compared to foreign currencies, the fluctuation in petroleum prices as a result of the unsettled Middle East, fiscal policy, and economic fluctuations. Each of these has ancillary effects on business forecasting and employment practices. Each also has an effect on the real Gross National Product, which *Fortune* predicts will continue to rise at an average rate of 2.6 percent through the year 2000.

    Fortune also predicts major demographic changes such as rising employment rates, greater personal wealth, and increased productivity. The rising employment rates predicted translate to an anticipated creation of some 13 million new jobs in the United States during the 1990's.[1] Such an economic climate make it more beneficial for U.S. businesses to subscribe to programs such as employment security. There are, however, a number of external factors that influence this decision. A few of these instrumental factors to consider include the following:

- U.S. Economy
- Competition
- Technological Change
- Unions

U.S. ECONOMY

In the early 1980's America experienced two successive recessions, then recovered to a modest productivity growth averaging 2.2 percent for the remainder of the 1980's. In the late 1980's and early 1990's the U.S. again experienced recessionary times. These cyclical swings in the economy have added to the confusion and complexity of workload planning. If workload planning were based on history and on the productivity gains that followed recessionary times in the past, the number of people employed would now be much different. According to research completed by *The Conference Board*, productivity has typically surged during recovery periods. They reported that in the post–World War II years, when recoveries lasted as long as the current recovery period, productivity growth rates ranged from 3.0 to 5.1 percent.[2] While recent productivity gains are somewhat less than those experienced during the post-World War II years, total employment has risen at a much higher rate. Much of this increased employment has required a job-skill mix unlike that experienced in the past. The majority of this job growth has taken place in the service sector, where required skills are varied and often more diverse than in manufacturing. As noted by *The Conference Board*, manufacturing recovered only 60 percent of the jobs lost during the recession that ended in the mid-1980's.

The Bureau of Labor Statistics confirmed this job-skill change in U.S. employment.

Basic manufacturing jobs peaked in 1979 at twenty one million jobs and have since declined by more than two million jobs. All of these factors—productivity improvements, skill-mix changes, and cyclical change in the economy—have added to the complexity of employment planning for corporations in national and global markets.

COMPETITION

Dynamic competitive pressures force meticulous workload planning strategies, and account for a number of challenges in managing workload and in maintaining an employment security practice. The goal for survival and success in the marketplace translates to the relentless pressure necessary to increase product demand, improve market share, focus on customer needs, and remain price-competitive. Each of these factors requires constant focus and management attention, as each is balanced with economic and market fluctuations.

An example of the impact of change on one major long-term employment security proponent is provided by Eastman Kodak. The company, an early practitioner, was often idealized for its commitment to employment security and protection against job loss. In the late 1970's sluggish sales, foreign competition, high costs, and lost market share shocked Kodak executives into abandonment of one of its most revered practices. It was forced to lay off employees in an attempt to resolve its financial crisis.

Other major U.S. companies have also resolved their reduced market capabilities and financial problems by releasing employees. For years management of these companies preached their commitment to employment security. Ken Olsen, president of Digital Equipment Corporation (DEC), talked to Wall Street analysts in 1982 and said that "when a company has a layoff, it's most often the management's fault. In a recession people want to test me, to see if I'm brave enough to have a layoff." Olsen went on to comment, "I'm willing to take that ridicule because it's paid off to hold onto our people." He continued, "we (DEC) have a big investment in the people . . . it's also good business for our people to have confidence that we will not lay them off just to help our profits short-term. This faith in the company is important."[3]

Digital Equipment Corporation practiced employment security for 34 years. In early 1991 DEC found it necessary to "involuntarily sever" approximately 3,500 employees in an attempt to remain competitive and profitable. Employees were not laid off in the normal sense; rather, DEC selected those that did not fit their immediate needs and future plans, paid them severance money, and released them to seek opportunity in other careers and companies.[4]

In the debate concerning competitiveness of U.S. business and employment security, a number of business executives have publicly stated the need to maintain a high-quality workforce. This workforce was often said to be the most important asset of the company. Public posture, however, often changed when competitive advantage and financial performance was at risk.

Employee layoffs in the United States continue to be the standard rather than the exception. This happens when company executives determine that the most expedient method in reacting to tactical cost problems is through immediate reduction of workforce. As an example, in 1984 the National Semiconductor Company listed job openings for 1,200 people at its Santa Clara site. In June 1985, a year later, the company laid off

1,300 employees, including 600 in the Santa Clara Valley, due in part to the effect of foreign and domestic competition.[5]

Within the scope of the competitive marketplace, the pressures brought by the assessment of being labor intensive and financially troubled, often result in a tactical response to a strategic problem. Employment security requires long-term planning and short-term strategies to manage effectively the cyclical and radical change that is the norm in American business.

TECHNOLOGICAL CHANGE

Technological change in the United States has resulted in plant closings, mass employee layoffs, and an overall decrease of production workers by 25 percent. The steel industry, for example, has declined from 600,000 workers in 1961 to fewer than 250,000 today. Automotive and other industries have experienced similar declines.

The United States has historically prized invention and felt secure with its technological leadership in the global economy. This feeling of security, however, is fading for many workers as recessionary times, combined with productivity improvements, have led to the demise of many jobs. The fear of "no worker" factories, although prophesied by some writers and management theorists, has not materialized. The propagation of robots into fully automatic, computer-controlled facilities has been slow. According to a study completed in March 1985 by the Congressional Research Service, the estimated cost to automate only five percent of the U.S. blue-collar workforce was projected to be greater than $45 billion. The study projected that although the United States is expected to make significant increases in robot investments for the remainder of this century, the investments might not be large enough to replace 5 percent of the blue-collar workforce.[6] In the service industries the need to boost productivity is also recognized. In the United States, capital investment in technology per worker averaged less than $450 per worker in the 1960's through the mid-1970's. By the mid-1980's, this figure jumped to over $1,000 per worker (in constant dollars).

The rate of technological change is somewhat slower than some have projected, yet permanent displacement of jobs continues to be a major concern for U.S. workers. This concern translates to fear of job obsolescence and often results in resistance to subsequent technological change. When improved technology is combined with economic fluctuations, an intense competitive environment, and productivity gains, employment security increases in importance for the workers and in degree of difficulty for management.

UNION INFLUENCES

The AFL-CIO's 1984 "Comparative Survey of Major Collective Bargaining Agreements" found that a small minority of contracts included no-layoff promises. The survey also revealed that 75 percent of surveyed contracts contained one or more worker protection clauses in the event of "major technological change, work transfer or closing either a department or plant." The contract language included promises of advanced notice of layoffs, commitments to preferred internal hiring, and establishment of retraining programs. The survey tracked 100 contracts, most in large bargaining units, covering both industrial and service sectors.[7]

Union organizations have a continuing interest in protecting their constituents from layoff. A recent study completed by the Work in America Institute stated that employment security

has become the *top* priority of American unions. According to an article in the *Harvard Business Review* this same union focus and negotiation has been the driving force for the adoption of employment security within the contractually protected workforce.[8] The range of protection offered by these contracts covers the continuum from jobs that are guaranteed for a specified period of time (i.e., the life of a contract), to union and management agreement that allows the union to examine company financial data and take an active part in the decision process prior to instituting employee layoff.

Historically, unions have experienced difficulty in obtaining employment security protection for their members and instead have accepted income security provisions such as unemployment benefits and early pensions. Union management's have discovered, however, that income security does not protect their workforce against the first law of American business, as one auto executive phrased it: "you get into trouble, you lay off people."

Union organizations are sometimes criticized for the effects that they are alleged to have on layoff and employee turnover rates. First, by raising wage levels unions reduce quits in a manner that standard theory would predict. Workers can express and resolve their differences internally rather than quit. The second effect of unions on turnover is to increase the layoff rate. The structure of union decision making places junior workers at a higher risk. "The consequence is a much higher layoff rate in unionized than in non-union firms."[9]

A study conducted by *The Conference Board* in 1980 provided insight into the importance of employment security and supported earlier findings that the first priority of unions was employment security for their members. Eighty employers whose workers had initiated proceedings to start unions were studied to determine the reasons that unions seemed attractive to the workers. The two most frequently reported reasons dealt with salary dissatisfaction and concern for employment security. The concern for employment security was mentioned by twenty-two of the eighty companies surveyed.[10]

Another example of the current union interest in employment security is found in the Fall 1987 labor contract negotiated between the United Auto Workers and the Ford Motor Company. The Ford contract provided a level of employment security by guaranteeing a fixed level of 104,000 jobs, unless sales slumped. A significant part of the contract contained the new guarantee that Ford keep one of every two jobs that it would have eliminated through attrition.[11] This contract was projected to cost Ford $700 per employee the first year, or a total of more than $70 million.

SUMMARY

In a free economy, employment security for workers can never be assured. Management and unions realize that a certain amount of employment insecurity accompanies economic vitality, the competitive marketplace, and technological change. The resistance to layoff by union and non-union employees, however, is based on the contention that the worker is often burdened with the entire risk and related problems, such as loss of medical benefits and life insurance, as a result of layoff.

The constant, and increasing, intensity brought about by economic pressures, national and global competition, technological change, and union organizations continue to challenge the most sincere commitment to employment security. The economic survival of a corporation has to be a top priority; however, layoffs sometime appear to provide resolution to tacti-

cal problems without consideration to long-term effects on employee morale, company loyalty, and impact on society.

NOTES

1. Michael Brody, "The 1990's," *Fortune*, 2 February 1987, 22.

2. Audrey Freedman, "Perspectives on Employment," *The Conference Board*, Research Bulletin #114, 1986, 7.

3. Tom Peters, *Thriving on Chaos* (New York: Harper and Row Publishers, 1988), 413.

4. Nell Margolis, "DEC to bite the layoff bullet," *Computer World*, 14 January 1991, 1.

5. 5. Richard Brandt, "Those Vanishing High-Tech Jobs," *Business Week*, 15 July 1985, 31.

6. *The Computer Revolution and the U.S. Labor Force*, Committee Print N. 99-G, prepared by Richard S. Belous for the House Subcommittee on oversight and investigations (Bethesda, Md.: Congressional Information Service, Inc., March 1985), 28.

7. "Comparative Survey of Major Collective Bargaining Agreements," Washington, D.C.: AFL-CIO Industrial Union Department, 1985.

8. Clyde W. Summers, "Protecting All Employees Against Unjust Dismissal," *Harvard Business Review*, January 1980, 133.

9. Richard B. Freeman and James L. Medoff, *What Do Unions Do?* (New York: Basic Books, 1984), 115

10. Fred J. Foulkes, "Employment Security," *Personnel Policies in Large Non-Union Companies* (Englewood Cliffs, N.J.: Prentice-Hall, 1980), 120.

11. Wendy Zellner and Aaron Bernstein, "Smiling Fender to Fender," *Business Week*, 5 October 1987, 39.

3
Company Loyalty and Employee Morale

Cost-cutting programs, such as the reduction of white-collar workers, are said to be changing the fabric of the American corporation. They threaten the concept of corporate loyalty: a real, if unwritten, social bond between employees and companies. Capturing the loyalty and commitment of hundreds or thousands of employees in an organization so that they direct their energies toward a common set of goals and objectives is an extremely difficult undertaking. According to one study completed by Greenhalgh, Lawrence, and Sutton, employee loyalty can be increased with company longevity. Their findings concluded that "senior employees typically have more organization-specific skills and greater loyalty."[1]

According to *Business Week* employee layoffs make financial sense in the short term. The cutbacks often cause stock prices to increase and affect after-tax savings. For example, by persuading 11,200 employees to leave voluntarily in 1985 the Du Pont

Company incurred a quarterly $125 million one-time charge but realized an annual after-tax savings of $230 million.[2]

Employees worry that their companies are becoming single-minded organizations that serve only one interest—Wall Street—says one twenty year veteran at Exxon Corporation who still has his job. "We used to be a community—employees, shareholders, lots of groups. We were committed to this company. We defended it back when people were accusing it of keeping tankers off over the horizon (to drive up the price of oil). Now it is clear that there is only one important group—the shareholders."[3]

A number of U.S. corporations are committed to the objective of operating with fewer white-collar workers. This objective is confirmed by a *Business Week* article that described a reduction of nearly one-half million white-collar workers in American corporations from 1984 to 1986. Some employees were gently coerced or convinced by attractive separation incentives; others were firmly pushed out the door.[4]

EXECUTIVE PERCEPTION

Japanese business executives contend that employment security has a positive effect on organization loyalty and is one of the keys to their high productivity. Their belief is supported by the number of Japanese companies that continue the practice today. U.S. business executives also prefer this level of loyalty but often believe that this is a luxury they cannot afford in today's competitive business world. More attention, however, is being paid by U.S executives and management consultants seeking supportive data that provide substantive facts regarding the effects of employment security on the workforce. Studies completed by management consultants over the last few years provide insight into these employee perceptions.

In late 1987 the management consulting group of Towers, Perrin, Forster, and Crosby Incorporated completed a study of 1,000 U.S. manufacturing and service employees in an attempt to ascertain the relationship between employment security and company loyalty. The study concluded that:

- 41 percent of those studied are concerned with employment security. This concern is caused by fears of corporate restructuring and foreign competition, and
- nearly a third of the participants said they would accept a job at the same pay with another company.[5]

A second group of studies was completed by the Hay Group of consultants. These studies focused on middle managers and professionals, and their satisfaction with and commitment to the companies that they worked for. The initial study was completed in 1977 and surveyed 1,600 companies. The results concluded that 88 percent of the middle managers and 72 percent of the professionals expressed satisfaction with their company. Nine years later, in 1986, a follow-up survey concluded that only 69 percent of middle management and a little over 50 percent of the professionals were satisfied with their company.[6] According to Michael Cooper, the president of Strategic Management Associates, a division of the Hay Group of consultants in Philadelphia, this decreased satisfaction with the company has a detrimental effect on job satisfaction and employee commitment (loyalty). Cooper writes that "employee commitment is declining more than it ever has, in the last decade." The surveys completed by the Hay Group provide a link between the drop in employee satisfaction and loyalty, and the decline in employment security that employees at all levels have experienced over the last decade.

THE CHALLENGE

A number of management theorists and business executives have concluded that primary objectives of business include profitability and longevity. The contention that often occurs between these objectives and employment security requires strong management commitment and an innovative approach to problem solving without impacting morale and loyalty, especially during cyclical times. A number of companies discontinued employment security over the last decade. During this same period some U.S. companies have been innovative in their approach to reduce excess workforce and match workload with available resources. U.S. executives have introduced a variety of programs to entice employees to voluntarily leave the business, or reduce available work hours.

PROGRAMS TO ADJUST WORKFORCE

A number of programs were introduced in an attempt to adjust workload to changing conditions with the intention to create minimal impact on employee morale and company loyalty. Some programs used in recent years to reduce or alter the workforce include the following:

- early retirement incentives whereby a person receives a sum of money for leaving the employ of the firm. These incentives range from one week's pay for each service year to four or more weeks' pay for each year of service,
- redeployment of resources; moving work to people or people to work,
- changes to appraisal measurement programs, thus seeking an increased number of management-initiated separations for unacceptable performance,

- forcing employees to take vacations or extended leaves with/without pay,
- shortened workweek at same/reduced pay,
- return of vended and subcontract work to provide additional in-house work for full-time employees,
- elimination of part-time and agency personnel, replacing these with trained/retrained full-time employees.

Each approach is thought to provide an acceptable alternative to employee layoff; however, each can negatively affect company loyalty and employee morale. As an example, the first program mentioned, early retirement incentives, would "seem to reveal an outmoded belief that older workers are less productive and less motivated than other workers, and are thus more expendable" according to the Work in America Institute study completed in 1984 by Jerome M. Rosow and Robert Zager.[7] Employees affected by such a program are usually a few years away from retirement and already feel insecure about the future. Many have given a lifetime of work to the company, along with commitment and loyalty, and can never feel certain as to when, or how, their career will be aborted. Companies that have offered early retirement incentives have expressed concern that employees they want to keep, those with marketable skills, are the first to leave. These programs, therefore, have to be managed with caution, and with an awareness of potential problems experienced in the aftermath.

OBSERVATION OF OTHERS

American companies have generally been unsuccessful in maintaining the planning process necessary to balance workload to employee headcount for many reasons. Sadami Wada, vice president of Sony Corporation of America, was quick to observe this and commented, "when I first came to the United States, I thought how convenient it was for American employers to be able to lay off people whenever business slumped." Wada soon changed his view. "Now I understand why some American companies fail to gain the loyalty and dedication of their employee. Employees cannot care for an employer who is prepared to take their livelihood away at the first sign of trouble."[8]

One American company that does not lay off employees "at the first sign of trouble" received tangible benefit for its treatment of employees, and has continued its employment security practice. Delta Air Lines demonstrated with conviction its belief that employees are their most important resource. It's continued a no-layoff policy since 1957. According to an article in *The Wall Street Journal*, Delta employees (in 1982), as thanks to the company for a salary increase and a no-layoff policy, raised enough money to buy the company a $30 million airplane.[9] Although this may be brushed off as an exception, it indicates that loyalty and commitment does evolve from the subtlety of positive employer and employee relations, and from the trust generated by employment security.

CONSEQUENCES OF REDUCTIONS

The anticipation of workforce reductions has an effect on employee morale and company loyalty, whether the layoffs actually take place or not. The fear of job loss has a "disastrous impact on people who have not lost their jobs, but are paralyzed by the fear that the next wave . . . could affect them," according to Leonard Greenhalgh, associate professor of Business Administration at Dartmouth College. This fear is complex, as it involves loss of income and benefits and also may mean, "losing status, contact with friends in the work place, privileges, flexibility, or subordinates."[10] According to Greenhalgh, these losses are possible even if employment per se is not in jeopardy. The employee fears losing the job as he or she presently knows it, causing an employment security crisis as depicted (see Figure 3.1). This crisis in turn can cause serious organizational problems such as reduced productivity, increased turnover, and resistance to change.

Figure 3.1

Causes and Consequences of a Job Security Crisis

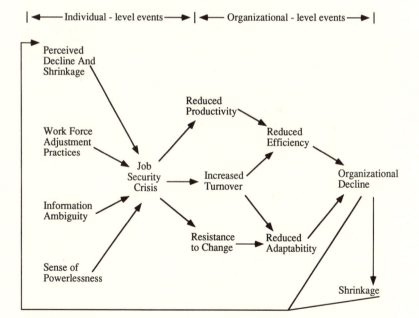

Source: Leonard Greenhalgh, *Human Resource Management,* Winter 1983, 433.
Reprinted by permission of John Wiley and Sons, Inc.

DATA AMBIGUITY

The results obtained from balancing financial expenditures with positive effects employment security has on company loyalty and employee morale remain uncertain and non-quantified. Past studies have not conclusively determined that the effects are positive or negative. The question still remains open regarding tangible conclusions drawn from this improved loyalty and morale. A number of unsubstantiated claims have been made that positively tie employment security with increases in company loyalty and employee morale. It can be implied from these that lower rates of absenteeism or length of service might be indicators of the success or failure of employment security. It is known that absenteeism has a direct affect on financial performance. Length of service can be linked to improved effectiveness and efficiency, based on the job-skill knowledge and business knowledge that employees accumulate over their work history.

This research effort is an attempt to explore both premises and compare companies that practice employment security with those that do not, to determine if indeed there are tangible as well as intangible benefits from increased company loyalty and employee morale.

COMPANY SELECTION

The relationship of employment security to company loyalty and employee morale was charted by examining employee absenteeism and employee length of service, two tangible measurements. Data was gathered from questionnaire responses collected from human resource executives of *Fortune* 500 industrial companies. Those twenty-three companies identified as practitioners (see Table 1.1) were matched with similar-sized

Fortune 500 companies in the same thirteen industries represented.

EXPECTATIONS

The questionnaire sought data to determine the relationship between employment security and company loyalty and employee morale and compare the effect, if any, on employee absenteeism and company length of service. Based on a number of statements made, and implied benefits discussed from such a practice, the expectations of these comparisons ranged from finding significant tangible benefits as a result of employment security to a rather subdued "hope it's at least as good" projection. The human resource executives surveyed responded in a more neutral tone and expected that there would be no significant difference when comparing employment secure companies with those not practicing, to determine the effect on employee absenteeism. The specific question asked was as follows:

The average annual absenteeism rate of employees in my company is:

_____ less than 3 percent
_____ 3 percent but less than 6 percent
_____ 6 percent but less than 9 percent
_____ 9 percent but less than 12 percent
_____ more than 12 percent

Thirty-six of 64 companies responded to this question; 15 of 23 that practice employment security and 21 of 41 that do not. Of the 13 industries represented in the study, only two industries failed to respond to the survey: chemicals and tobacco. The responses received for the question on absenteeism are shown in Table 3.1.

Table 3.1

Employment Secure and Non-Employment Secure Companies
Relationship of Employment Security to Absenteeism

Percentage	<3	3<6	6<9	9<12	>12
Employment Secure	5	9	-	1	-
Percent Responses	33%	60%	-	7%	-
Non–Employment Secure	8	11	2	-	-
Percent Responses	38%	52%	10%	-	-

Source: Questionnaire returns

Seeking data on employee length of service, a similar set of questions were asked of human resource executives for those same companies. The first, a general question, sought the professional opinion of whether employment security would indeed be a significant factor in increasing the average length of employee service for a company. The consensus from executives representing both groups was that there would be no significant difference. These executives were then asked a more specific question in an attempt to quantify their earlier response. The question asked was as follows:

The average length of service of employees in my company is:

_____ less than five years
_____ five but less than ten years
_____ ten but less than fifteen years
_____ fifteen but less than twenty years
_____ more than twenty years.

The same thirty-six companies again responded; 65 percent of those surveyed companies that practice employment security and 51 percent of those that do not. The responses received are shown in Table 3.2.

Some caution must be exercised because of the number of companies responding. The responses, however, provide a base from which conclusions can be drawn, or at minimum, a foundation that can be established for future studies.

DATA ANALYSIS

Data received from the questionnaire provided more information than that shown for the two questions, and sought both objective and subjective information from the human resource executives. The quantitative data shown, however, was used to compare both groups of companies to determine the statistical significance, based on a level of significance of 0.05. The t-test was used for these analyses.

Table 3.2

**Employment Secure and Non–Employment Secure Companies
Relationship of Employment Security to Length of Service**

Years of Service	<5	5<10	10<15	15<20	>20
Employment Secure	-	4	9	1	1
Percent Responses	-	26%	60%	7%	7%
Non–Employment Secure	4	3	10	2	2
Percent Responses	19%	14%	47%	10%	10%

Source: Questionnaire returns

EMPLOYEE ABSENTEEISM

The statistical analysis of responses on employee absenteeism determined that there is no significant difference between those practicing employment security and those that do not. The results agreed with the perceptions of human resource executives. The results, if accepted, quell the critics who claim that employment security breeds complacency because of a reduced fear of job loss, and reduces the enthusiasm of proponents that claim increased morale and company loyalty would lead to lower employee absenteeism, all other factors being equal. Although the results must be interpreted with caution it is recognized that a number of other factors related to employee absenteeism were not included as part of this analysis. These include average worker age, stress, type of work performed, and management policies and practices.

LENGTH OF SERVICE

Employee length of service was examined for those companies that practice employment security, and those that do not. The length of time a company had been operating is also relevant; therefore, a question was asked the survey recipients to make certain data comparison would be meaningful and consistent. The responses received showed no significant difference between the two groups, when comparing length of time in business.

The analysis of responses for employee length of service also found no significant difference between the two groups. These results agreed with perceptions of human resource executives surveyed. Some of these, however, were apologetic for their response and a few executives from companies practicing employment security noted that recent company growth, and subsequent hiring, reduced average length of service in their companies. In an effort to confirm this phenomenon, accumulative employment and sales data were compiled for those companies responding to the survey, providing they attained the *Fortune* 500 listing for each of the years from 1978 to 1987. This data is shown in Table 3.3.

IMPLICATIONS

The results of this study indicate that employment security does not have a significant effect on employee absenteeism or company length of service. Employee morale and company loyalty, however, are strengthened by the practice, according to a number of studies and executive interviews. The most visible survey and results are from the Work in America Institute study referred to previously.

Data in Table 3.3 support comments made by human resource executives of employment-secure companies. These companies were indeed hiring new employees over the time period studied, increasing their number of employees by 26.3 percent, which would tend to lower the average length of service for those companies. During the same period from 1978 to 1987 the non–employment-secure companies reduced their average population by 7.2 percent.

Assuming that less senior employees would be the first to be released, employee reduction would tend to decrease the average length of service. This data is supported by the response received from another question in the survey asking whether the company was unionized. Union organizations typically lay off employees based on date of hire, with the most recent hires released first. It was determined that companies with unions were less apt to practice employment security than those not

Table 3.3

Employees and Sales Revenue, 1978–1987: Companies Responding to Survey

	Y/E 1978	Y/E 1987	% Change
Employment Secure			
Number of Employees	747,513	944,357	
Average Number of Employees	67,956	85,851	+26.3%
Change in Average Number		+17,895	
Annual Sales (Millions)	$95,384.9	$172,544.7	
Average Sales/Company	8,671.4	15,685.9	+80.9%
Change in Average Sales		+7,014.5	
Non-Employment Secure			
Number of Employees	670,538	622,209	
Average Number of Employees	74,504	69,134	-7.2%
Change in Average Number		-5,370	
Annual Sales (Millions)	$59,780.2	$105,477.4	
Average Sales/Company	6,642.2	11,719.7	+76.4%
Change in Average Sales		+5,077.5	

Source: Questionnaire and *Fortune* 500

unionized. This could be interpreted to show that security might be considered a preventive act by management to keep unions out. It could also be interpreted that non-union companies offer employment security as one of a number of programs leading to more satisfied employees and a reduction in the need to organize and gain recognition and protection usually associated with union membership.

Employee morale and company loyalty are two important, and difficult to measure, components professed to be advantages realized from a no-layoff policy. The long-term commitment and management expectations need to address challenge offered by cyclical change.

The largest U.S. corporation that successfully employs a no-layoff policy is IBM. This practice requires commitment from all levels of management in IBM and is often mentioned and openly discussed by John Akers, president of IBM. In May 1987 Mr. Akers told an audience at Harvard University that "if IBM has a monopoly, it's in the way it manages its people." Referring directly to IBM's employment security practice he said that in the long run the practice enables IBM to attract and hold very fine people.[11] The high marks that IBM employees provide on annual opinion survey questionnaires for morale and loyalty attest to the strong acceptance and approval of IBM's commitment.

Financial implications that U.S. executives fear because of such a practice present a differing set of questions and concerns. These will be explored, along with a search for tangible costs and benefits resulting from employment security.

NOTES

1. Leonard Greenhalgh, Anne T. Lawrence, and Robert I. Sutton, "Determinants of Workforce Reduction Strategies in Declining Organizations," Academy of Management Review, Spring 1988, 247.

2. Bruce Nussbaum, "The End of Corporate Loyalty," *Business Week*, 4 August 1986, 43.

3. Ibid., 44.

4. Ibid., 42.

5. Ibid.

6. Amanda Bennett, "Growing Small," *The Wall Street Journal*, 4 May 1987, 20.

7. Jerome M. Rosow and Robert Zager, *Employment Security in a Free Economy* (New York: Pergamon Press, 1984), 115.

8. James F. Bolt, "Job Security: Its Time Has Come," *Harvard Business Review*, November–December 1983, 118.

9. Margaret Loeb, "Staid Delta Air Tries to Stem Losses by Following Other Carriers' Moves," *The Wall Street Journal*, 6 September 1983, 29.

10. Leonard Greenhalgh, "Managing the Job Insecurity Crisis," *Human Resource Management*, Winter 1983, 432.

11. D. Quinn Mills, *The IBM Lesson*, (New York: Times Books, 1988), 216.

4
Financial Performance

Employee morale and company loyalty are sometimes referred to as the "lifeline" of an organization. If this is so, financial performance might be considered the "heartbeat." Many decisions center around past financial performance, present performance, and strategic outlook. Because of this, organizations often have difficulty focusing on programs that do not have a direct positive impact on that financial performance. Often pressures from investors, stockholders, boards of directors, and special interest groups for improvement of quarterly earnings preclude this focus. Based on past actions and general lack of management commitment, employment security is one area in need of that focus. The management challenge is to quantify financial benefits for organizations that practice employment security, and cultivate management desire and commitment to provide that security. This analysis accepts that challenge, and is an attempt to substantiate that relationship and provide management with an alternative to employee layoff while maintaining financial success.

HISTORICAL PERSPECTIVE

Key events have occurred in recent years that affect the no-layoff decision for U.S. business. These events have reaffirmed the need to evaluate a no-layoff practice and determine the relationship of employment security to financial performance. These two factors, financial performance and employment security, are sometimes seen as mutually exclusive and contentious terms. A few companies, however, treat them as congruent entities that lead to longevity and success for an organization.

According to a recent article, four phenomena in the United States have made employment security an important practice for us to understand. They are:

1. the prolonged economic downturn beginning in the mid-1970's (which) resulted in the highest rates of job loss since the Great Depression of the 1930's,
2. an upsurge of mergers and acquisitions since the mid-1960's,
3. a rapidly changing industrial structure—from a predominantly manufacturing economy to a service economy, and from the predominance of basic industries to the rise of high-technology industries,
4. the trend toward decreasing union representation of the U.S workforce . . . (because of this) an increasing number of workers are vulnerable to the effects of unilateral decisions from which they have little recourse.[1]

These phenomena continue to threaten employment security and are viewed by workers as some degree of job insecurity.

Any reduction or change in workload requirements force management to evaluate factors and decide whether to lay off employees or to retain, retrain, and redeploy them to other positions within the company. Each of these decisions represents a cost to the organization and is therefore analyzed for short- and long-term effect on financial performance.

A number of management professionals have presented the premise that all assets of an organization must be managed and protected to effectively control costs and expenses. Employment security is one such program that is said to protect the assets of the corporation. Commenting on this was Dr. Sheldon Weinig, chairman and chief executive officer of Materials Research Corporation. Dr Weinig stated that "people are very expensive assets, and you should always protect the assets of the company."[2] People are protected at Materials Research Corporation, which has never resorted to employee layoff.

The proponents of employment security write that the protection of jobs is necessary to establish and maintain financial performance, which is the end result of well-executed management plans and strategies. Critics write that employment security is expensive, unnecessary, and can decimate a financially vibrant organization.

RECENT STUDIES

A number of studies have reviewed and analyzed the relationship of employment security to financial performance. In one study, it was "demonstrated that long term costs of layoffs exceeded those of natural attrition in a declining public sector organization." It was projected that these same findings could generalize to private sector settings as well.[3] The study reconfirmed that little is known about costs and benefits of workforce reduction except that a number of problems arise as a result of employment insecurity. In addition to the expenses of severance pay, higher unemployment compensation taxes, and continuation of health insurance and other benefits for a period after the layoff, other costs are incurred. They include administrative and legal costs, the expense of rehiring and training workers when demand resumes, and outplacement fees, all of which add up to a staggering burden that could substantially reduce financial gains made in cutting the workforce. For example, one company spent more than $50 million in severance pay and benefits as a result of employee layoffs.[4]

Another study concluded that employment security "enables a firm to be more productive . . . increases the competitiveness and wealth of society . . . and helped create a huge new (computer) industry with hundreds of thousands of good jobs."[5] Manifestations such as this are prevalent, sometimes vague, and difficult to isolate with substantive proof supportive to proponents of employment security.

Fred Foulkes, director of the Human Resources Policy Institute at the School of Management at Boston University, contends that costs associated with employment security are substantial. Foulkes states that for a variety of reasons it is not possible to conclude whether the benefits actually exceed the costs for any particular company.[6] Foulkes does, however, write that advantages of employment security include lower turnover rates, which contribute to lower costs. Employee turnover rates for practicing companies are said to be a fraction of the national figure.[7]

Quantitative proof that employment security is either financially beneficial or detrimental to profits has not yet been determined. This analysis is an attempt to provide financial evidence by comparing net income as a percentage of sales, assets, and equity of companies that practice employment security with those that do not.

PROBLEM AND CHALLENGE

The short-term management focus on quarterly profits of an organization requires quick analyses during cyclical periods. This short-term outlook may be changing, according to Gary B. Hansen, professor of economics, Utah State University, and director of the Utah Center for Productivity and Quality of Working Life. Hansen writes that "evidence from the recessions of the past decade suggests that the practice of laying off workers is itself costly . . . those that experimented with alternatives to worker layoff during this period discovered that these (alternative) measures could in fact help them regain economic stability and increase productivity."[8] Although supportive evidence is noted, executive management within U.S. corporations seem reluctant to change, as evidenced from past actions. Layoffs continue to dominate the news, especially during recessionary times, as experienced in the 1980's and early 1990's. Some see employees as being exploited and mishandled by business. As an example, Leonard Greenhalgh writes that "the unneeded human capital is written off in much the same way that plants and equipment are written off." He continues, "since labor has no salvage value, disposal tends to be a simple question of expediency."[9]

In another article, Greenhalgh, Lawrence, and Sutton note the negative effect that employment security has on the financial performance due to "waiting for employees to leave through attrition . . . (when they) are no longer required. Inducements to stimulate attrition . . . also drain the organization of needed cash. Transfers within the organization can be costly because employees are paid full wages . . . when they are moving or adjusting to new jobs."[10]

These studies and statements by experts and intellectuals indicate that the affect that employment security has on financial performance is implied and differs, but is not substantiated by factual evidence.

PERCEPTION AND ANALYSIS

The perception of some is expressed by the "silent majority" that neither comments nor writes about a "no-layoff" society. There are a number of examples that cite success in U.S. business, and there is no shortage of articles that are critical when one of the major corporate practitioners of employment security announces involuntary (or even voluntary) employee reduction programs. A case in point is a voluntary employee separation plan announced by International Business Machines Corporation (IBM) on March 28, 1991. The news media added their interpretation to IBM press releases and stated over national news networks that IBM was laying off 10,000 to 16,000 people in an effort to streamline operations. An IBM voluntary employee reduction program was once again misinterpreted by the press. Media sometimes overreact and write "I told you so" articles when employment security falters, often with more gusto than when non-job secure companies announce massive involuntary separations.

One common perception of employment security is that it nurtures mediocrity and complacency in the workplace. Some point to government jobs as an example. The Work in America study noted that when an organization increases employment security for employees, "the performance of that organization is increased."[11] Another study correlated managerial practices with a five-year average annual rate in profits and found that profit growth was lowest when employment security was either very high or very low. The researchers offered the following explanation: "when job security is too high, performance problems tend to be ignored; where job security is too low, employees see little opportunity for personal growth and career development."[12]

Management perception is difficult to change. Many U.S. managers continue to subscribe to employee layoff and are not receptive to a change in that philosophy. Corporate plans, practices, policies, and strategies are generally not focused on managing employment security, especially during economic cycles and business downturns in which financial performance is already stressed.

SCOPE OF STUDY

The level of an organization's financial performance is a key measurement of success or failure. Without a high degree of financial success the survival of the organization is jeopardized.

Fortune and other business periodicals commonly use net income as a percentage of sales, assets, and equity as a measure of a company's financial performance. These relationships are accepted criteria for completing a comparative analysis, are accepted as financial business indicators, and will be used in the comparison of data for the ten-year period 1978–1987. The level of significance was established at 0.05. Data was analyzed using t-tests for industry-to-industry and for year-to-year comparisons between the two groups.

The total population of *Fortune* 500 companies was considered for this analysis. From this population, the twenty-three companies identified as practitioners of employment security were selected and matched (based on similar number of employees) with twenty-three companies not practicing employment security. These forty-six companies are distributed among the thirteen industries as shown in Table 4.1.

Table 4.1

Industry Representation and Number of Companies in Each

Industry	Number of Companies
Aerospace	2
Chemicals	2
Computers	14
Electronics	4
Forest Products	2
Furniture	2
Metals	4
Motor Vehicles	2
Petroleum	2
Pharmaceutical	4
Scientific and Photographic	4
Soap and Cosmetic	2
Tobacco	2
Total Companies Compared	46

Source: *A Review and Evaluation of Employment Security Practices,* 189.

DATA COLLECTION AND MEASUREMENT

Financial data and number of employees was gathered from *Fortune* in their annual report of the top 500 industrial corporations. Questionnaires were mailed to each participating company in an attempt to obtain additional data from human resource executives. This data was used to interpret and support financial data gathered. Both data sources were used for an industry-by-industry and year-to-year analysis, comparing those that practice employment security with those that do not.

SELECTION PROCESS FOR INDUSTRY-BY-INDUSTRY ANALYSIS

In the industry-by-industry analysis it was determined that not all companies selected for this study attained the *Fortune* 500 list for all ten years. A selection process was designed to match companies in each industry and provide data integrity and consistency.

When the industry was represented by one company practicing employment security, and one that does not (aerospace, chemicals, forest products, furniture, motor vehicles, petroleum, soap and cosmetics, and tobacco), it was required that both be included in the *Fortune* 500 list for a given year or industry data for that year was not included in the study.

When the industry was represented by two or more companies practicing employment security (computers, electronics, metals, pharmaceutical, and scientific and photographic) at least one company practicing employment security and one that does not were required to be listed in the *Fortune* 500 in order for that years's data to be included in the industry-by-industry analysis.

The selection process explained for this analysis provided the following results (see Table 4.2):
- ten industries with ten years of data
- one industry with nine years of data

- one industry with seven years of data
- one industry with three years of data

Table 4.2

**Number of Years Data Per Industry
Industry-by-Industry Analysis**

Industries with 10 years of data:
> Aerospace
> Chemicals
> Computers
> Electronics
> Motor Vehicles
> Petroleum
> Pharmaceutical
> Scientific and Photographic
> Soap Products
> Tobacco

Industry with 9 years of data
> Metals

Industry with 7 years of data:
> Forest Products

Industry with 3 years of data:
> Furniture

Source: *A Review and Evaluation of Employment Security Practices,* 72.

Note: All 13 industries are represented in this industry-by-industry analysis.

SELECTION PROCESS FOR YEAR-TO-YEAR ANALYSIS

For the year-to-year analysis, comparative annual data for companies that practice employment security was matched with those that do not. To maintain data consistency, the selection process criteria required that each company be listed on the *Fortune* 500 for each of the ten years from 1978 to 1987. When a company did not achieve the listing for any one of the ten years they were excluded from the year-to-year analysis. This selection process reduced the employment-secure companies from twenty-three to seventeen, and the non-practicing companies from twenty-three to thirteen. The remaining thirty companies, representing ten industries, are shown in Table 4.3.

RESULTS FROM INDUSTRY-BY-INDUSTRY ANALYSIS

The results obtained from the industry-by-industry analysis will be reviewed in three segments by comparing companies that practice employment security (by industry) with those that do not to determine the level of significance for differences in:
- net income as a percentage of sales,
- net income as a percentage of assets, and
- net income as a percentage of equity.

The opinion of forty-one human resource executives responding to the questionnaire was that there would not be a significant difference between these two groups in net income as a percentage of sales, assets, and equity. The consensus was that employment security would not provide financial advantage for those that do not practice, nor would the practice be detrimental to the corporate profits of those practicing companies.

Table 4.3

Companies in the Year-to-Year Analysis

Industry	Employment Secure	Non–Empl. Secure
Aerospace	Boeing Corporation	McDonnell Douglas
Chemicals	E. I. Du Pont	Dow Chemical
Computers	Control Data	Gould Corporation
	Data General	NCR Corporation
	DEC	
	Hewlett-Packard	
	IBM	
	Pitney-Bowes	
Electronics	Motorola	Westinghouse
Motor Vehicles	Dana Corporation	Borg-Warner Company
Petroleum	Exxon Corporation	Mobil Oil Company
Pharmaceutical	Eli Lilly	Merck Industries
	Upjohn Corporation	Smithkline-Beckman
Scientific and	3M Corporation	Eastman Kodak
Photographic	Tektronix	General Signal
Soap Products	Avon Products	Colgate-Palmolive
Tobacco	R. J. Reynolds	Philip Morris

Source: *A Review and Evaluation of Employment Security Practices*,
    73.

Note: All 30 companies were listed on the *Fortune* 500 for each of the
ten years 1978–1987.

    For each year the arithmetic mean of the three measures of
financial performance of the employment secure companies were
compared with the arithmetic mean of those not practicing
employment security.

Net Income as a Percentage of Sales

The industry-by-industry analysis (see Table 4.4) of net income to sales for the thirteen industries indicate no significant difference between those that practice employment security and those that do not for three industries (chemicals, electronics, and tobacco), and a significant difference for the remaining ten industries studied. A more detailed analysis of these ten industries indicates that companies practicing employment security reported a significantly lower ratio of net income to sales in two of the industries (motor vehicles and pharmaceuticals).

In the remaining eight industries (aerospace, computers, forest products, furniture, metals, petroleum, scientific and photographic, and soap and cosmetic) the companies that practice employment security reported a significantly higher ratio of net income to sales. Although the results are inclusive, those companies that practice employment security enjoyed a significantly higher ratio of net income to sales in eight of thirteen industries, with no significant difference in three of the remaining five industries.

Net Income as a Percentage of Assets

The analysis of the thirteen industries for net income as a percentage of assets yielded similar results. There was no significant difference between companies that practice employment security and those that do not for six industries (chemicals, electronics, furniture, motor vehicles, petroleum, and tobacco). One industry (pharmaceutical) reported a significantly lower ratio, and the remaining six industries (aerospace, computers, forest products, metals, scientific and photographic, and soap and cosmetic) reported a significantly higher ratio (see Table 4.4).

Table 4.4

**Industry-by-Industry Analysis
Employment Secure and Non–Employment Secure Company
Data, 1978–1987**

Net Income as a Percentage of:

Industry	Sales t Value	Assets t Value	Equity t Value	Derived t Value
Aerospace	3.533	3.096	2.709	1.833
Chemicals	1.073	0.417	0.447	1.833
Computers	6.433	5.212	0.588	1.833
Electronics	0.994	0.141	0.749	1.833
Forest Products	3.848	3.869	2.942	1.943
Furniture	3.600	1.097	0.540	2.920
Metals	4.991	4.743	4.458	1.860
Motor Vehicles	2.570	0.781	0.121	1.833
Petroleum	6.801	0.293	2.035	1.833
Pharmaceutical	3.997	5.920	3.162	1.833
Scientific	2.194	3.207	3.433	1.833
Soap and Cosmetic	2.797	1.976	2.067	1.833
Tobacco Products	1.584	0.652	1.404	1.833

Note: level of significance = 0.05

Data: *Fortune* 500 Annual Listings of U.S. Companies

The results were again inclusive. However, those companies represented that practice employment security enjoyed a significantly higher ratio of net income to assets in six of thirteen industries, with no significant difference in six of the remaining seven industries.

Net Income as a Percentage of Equity

Analysis of the thirteen industries for net income as a percentage of equity provided the following results. There was no significant difference between companies that practice employment security and those that do not for six industries (chemicals, computers, electronics, furniture, motor vehicles, and tobacco). One industry (pharmaceutical) reported a significantly lower percentage, and the remaining six industries (aerospace, forest products, metals, petroleum, scientific and photographic, and soap and cosmetic) reported a significantly higher ratio of net income to equity (see Table 4.4).

The results shown are inconclusive. However, those companies that practice employment security enjoyed a significantly higher ratio of net income to equity in six of thirteen industries and no significant difference in six of the remaining seven industries.

CONCLUSIONS FROM INDUSTRY-BY-INDUSTRY ANALYSIS

Each of thirteen industries was analyzed in an attempt to discern whether companies that practice employment security are in fact financially impacted by additional costs. When comparing net income as a percentage of sales, assets, and equity for the two groups—those that practice employment security and those that do not—it was determined that of thirty-nine distinct comparisons there was no significance difference for fifteen of those. Of the remaining twenty-four comparisons, twenty indicated that those companies that practice employment security reported a significantly higher percentage of net income to sales, assets, or equity. The remaining four comparisons indicate that companies that do not practice employment security reported ignificantly lower percentages of net income to sales, assets, or equity (see Table 4.5).

Table 4.5

Net Income as a Percentage of Sales, Assets, Equity
Industry-by-Industry Analysis Summary
Employment Secure and Non–Employment Secure Company
Data, 1978–1987

Significant Difference

Industry	Sales	Assets	Equity
Aerospace	Yes	Yes	Yes
Chemicals	No	No	No
Computers	Yes	Yes	No
Electronics	No	No	No
Forest Products	Yes	Yes	Yes
Furniture	Yes	No	No
Metals	Yes	Yes	Yes
Motor Vehicles	Yes	No	No
Petroleum	Yes	No	Yes
Pharmaceutical	Yes	Yes	Yes
Scientific	Yes	Yes	Yes
Soap and Cosmetic	Yes	Yes	Yes
Tobacco Products	No	No	No

Note: level of significance = 0.05

Source: *A Review and Evaluation of Employment Security Practices,* 136.

CONCLUSIONS FROM YEAR-TO-YEAR ANALYSIS

The year-to-year analysis was also reviewed in three segments by comparing companies that practice employment security (by year) with those that do not, to ascertain whether there are significant differences in:

- net income as a percentage of sales,
- net income as a percentage of assets, and
- net income as a percentage of equity.

Data gathered from human resource executives responding to the questionnaire, representing both groups, indicated that they expected no significant difference in these ratios. The consensus of these executives was that employment security would not provide a financial advantage for those that do not practice, nor would an employment security practice be detrimental to corporate profits. In this comparison seventeen companies practicing employment security were compared with thirteen that do not, for the ten-year period 1978–1987. For each year the arithmetic mean of each of the three measures of financial performance was compared for the two groups.

The results of the year-to-year analysis are shown in Table 4.6. The data indicates that, for each year in the ten-year period, there was no significant difference in either net income as a percentage of sales or net income as a percentage of assets, between the employment secure and the non–employment secure companies. For net income as a percentage of equity, there was a significant difference between the two groups in only one year (1978). The reason for this deviation was not readily apparent. Hence, the belief that there is no difference in financial performance between companies that practice employment security and those that do not, was supported.

Table 4.6

**Year-to-Year Summary
Employment Secure and Non–Employment Secure Company
Data, 1978–1987**

Net Income as a Percentage of:

Year	Sales t Value	Assets t Value	Equity t Value	Derived t Value
1978	1.265	1.358	2.128	1.701
1979	0.513	1.299	1.405	1.701
1980	1.074	0.686	0.414	1.701
1981	0.257	0.377	0.010	1.701
1982	0.111	0.231	0.596	1.701
1983	0.107	0.059	0.450	1.701
1984	0.973	0.398	1.114	1.701
1985	0.167	0.711	0.022	1.701
1986	0.070	0.070	1.063	1.701
1987	0.323	0.236	0.810	1.701

Note: level of significance = 0.05

The 17 employment secure and 13 non–employment secure companies
represent 10 industries: aerospace, chemicals, computers, electronics,
motor vehicles, petroleum, pharmaceutical, scientific and photo
graphic, soap and cosmetic, and tobacco.

Data: *Fortune* 500

IMPLICATIONS DRAWN FROM ANALYSIS OF FINANCIAL PERFORMANCE

This segment of the study found that, on the average, the
financial performance of employment secure companies did not

differ significantly from those not practicing this security. These results lend support to the proponents of employment security. The findings suggest that firms may provide their employees with employment security without jeopardizing their financial performance *vis-a'-vis* firms that do not have such a policy. The implications of this conclusion are enormous for management, employees, stockholders, and society.

Companies that provide job security may reap the benefits of a motivated and flexible workforce (claimed by advocates of job security) without suffering financial disadvantage. At the same time, society would not be confronted with the problems of large-scale layoffs.

CAUTIONARY NOTE

These findings need to be viewed with some caution. The data did not demonstrate that a policy of job security leads to, or brings about, better or poorer company financial results. It is recognized that other variables affect financial performance.

Second, the study focused on a relatively small number of large industrial firms in a limited number of industries. Hence the findings may not be applicable to small industrial firms, to firms in other industries, or to non-industrial companies. In addition, while the measures of financial performance used in the study are standard indicators used in financial analyses, performance of the firms could have been assessed by other financial measures, raising the possibility that different results might have been obtained.

NOTES

1. Leonard Greenhalgh and Zehava Rosenblatt, "Job Security: Toward Conceptual Clarity," *Academy of Management Review*, Vol. 9, No. 3, 1984, 438.

2. Jocelyn F. Gutchess, *Employment Security in Action: Strategies That Work* (New York: Pergamon Press, 1985), 19.

3. Leonard Greenhalgh, Anne T. Lawrence, and Robert I. Sutton, "Determinants of Workforce Reduction Strategies in Declining Organizations," *Academy of Management Review*, Spring 1988, 251.

4. James F. Bolt, "Job Security: Its Time Has Come," *Harvard Business Review*, November–December 1983, 122.

5. Jerome M. Rosow and Robert Zager, *Employment Security in a Free Economy* (New York: Pergamon Press, 1984), 80.

6. Fred K. Foulkes, "Employment Security," *Personnel Policies in Large Non-Union Companies* (Englewood Cliffs, N.J.: Prentice-Hall, 1980), 118–119.

7. Fred K. Foulkes and Anne Whitman, "Marketing Strategies to Maintain Full Employment," *Harvard Business Review*, July–August 1985, 32.

8. Gary B. Hansen, "Preventing Layoffs: Developing an Effective Job Security and Economic Adjustment Program," *U.S. Department of Labor BLMR 102*, Bureau of Labor-Management Relations and Cooperative Programs, Washington, D.C., 1986, 1.

9. Leonard Greenhalgh, "Maintaining Organizational Effectiveness During Organizational Retrenchment," *The Journal of Applied Behavioral Science*, Vol. 18, No. 2, 1982, 156.

10. Leonard Greenhalgh, Anne T. Lawrence, and Robert I. Sutton, "Determinants of Workforce Reduction Strategies in Declining Organizations," *Academy of Management Review*, Spring 1988, 248.

11. Jerome Rosow and Robert Zager, *Employment Security in a Free Economy* (New York: Pergamon Press, 1984), 80.

12. George G. Gordon and Bonnie Goldberg, "Is There a Climate for Success," *Management Review* 66, May 1977, 42–43.

5
Employee Productivity

Productivity measurements in American industry have been calculated, compared, and utilized as one of the key indicators for analyzing success or failure of business within the U.S. economy. The measurement is used at the macro and the micro level, at the international and national level, at the federal government and state government level, and at the chief executive and supervisor level. As a measurement tool it is sometimes used to provide "bragging rights." As a control mechanism it is utilized in a variety of ways, from promoting federal legislation for capital investment tax credits to the nudging of employees for a more robust generation of outputs. The measurement of productivity is a valuable tool, often quoted, sometimes misunderstood and misrepresented, and universally accepted as a representative relative measurement of progress, or lack thereof.

A number of factors are said to influence productivity. It is impossible and impractical to isolate one or two of these. However, it has been stated that employment security practices have an effect on the economic productivity of organizations and, according to the Academy of Management Journal, "in business organizations the primary goal is economic productivity."[1] This economic productivity is enhanced through employment security, according to the Work in America study, which notes that "the performance enhancements made possible by such a commitment (of employment security) will help pay for increased security against business declines and will strengthen employee commitment to increase the company's edge and market share."[2]

A strong bias, however, remains in the sociology literature toward believing that turnover is negatively correlated with performance. According to Paul Osterman, "the origins of this bias lie, first, in the equating of performance with productivity, not profits; second, in the view that work group cohesion depends on stability; and third, in the view that the best workers are those most likely to leave."[3] Osterman, from his observation and research, writes that if performance is indeed measured as work-group productivity, then it appears possible to conclude that performance improves as turnover is reduced. Many would argue that the social benefits exceed private benefits. Turnover statistics, both quits and layoffs, are very unevenly distributed by age, sex, industry and occupation because:

- women have higher quit rates than men,
- younger workers have higher quit rates than older workers, and
- layoffs are concentrated in blue-collar manufacturing sectors (although these numbers are becoming more broadly distributed among white-collar and non-manufacturing).[4]

Most major U.S. firms treat productivity and employment security as opposites rather than complements according to

Marta Mooney, a professor at Fordham University. She writes that management typically desires productivity, and avoids the issue of employment security, while assuming that employees want employment security and avoid productivity.[5]

Employment security is said to be the cause of conflicting perceptions regarding benefits and costs between advocates and critics, and management and employees, adding to the confusion. Ms. Mooney writes that employment security increases productivity, which she claims is consistent with behavioral theory and associated research that has been completed. The example used by Ms. Mooney is the theory of motivation developed by American psychologist Abraham Maslow. She writes that Maslow holds that employee motivation is explained by a more or less stable hierarchy of needs, which employment security addresses to some extent.[6] She notes that while the critics point to highly protected civil servants as being counted among the least productive employee group in America, employees whose jobs are threatened are often considered to be among the most productive. Mooney says that this contradiction can be resolved by combining evidence from both sides—the highly protected and the highly threatened—and has graphically portrayed her argument in Figure 5.1, which implies that most organizations are better off with a well-designed employment security practice than without one. However, the balance of too much or too little security must be a consideration in weighing costs and benefits.

RECENT STUDIES

Several studies have demonstrated a positive correlation between employment security and employee productivity. One such study, conducted at Boston University by Fred Foulkes,

Figure 5.1

Productivity and Job Security

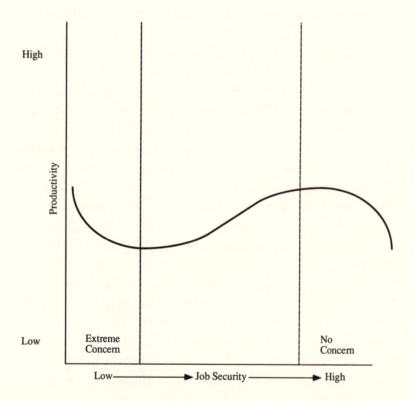

Source: Marta Mooney, *Personnel Administrator*, January 1984, 44. Reprinted with permission from *HR Magazine* (formerly *Personnel Administrator*) published by the Society for Human Resource Management, Alexandria, VA.

found that offering employment security builds employee loyalty to the company, confidence and trust in management, lowers staff turnover, and improves employee relations—all competitive advantages that contribute to higher productivity and profits.[7] Companies that practice employment security, such as the forty-seven companies cited by the Work in America Institute (see Table 1.1), report that employees are receptive to—even enthusiastic about—productivity improvements and new technology because they know they will not lose their jobs as a result of productivity improvements.

James Bolt, president of Human Resources Associates of Westport, Connecticut, writes that of all the factors arguing in favor of employment security, the single overriding benefit is increased productivity. At a time when the United States needs to increase productivity, employment insecurity for the vast majority of workers, "stands as a major impediment . . . no amount of technological innovation, worker education and training, work force restrictions, or job redesign can realize its full productivity improvement potential without the cooperation of trusting employees . . . who know that change in the work place does not threaten their livelihood."[8]

A study completed by Richard Pascale found that Japanese firms that operate manufacturing facilities in the United States, and that have adopted employment security, perform better than comparable U.S. firms—with higher productivity and profits.[9] This finding is also supported by an IBM executive who describes his belief in the connection between employment security and productivity when he observed the following: "Our (IBM) people . . . have cut two-thirds of the hours that go into manufacturing our product. The cost of the product went down 45 percent during a ten-year period when wages vastly increased . . . much of the commitment stems from the security they (employees) know is theirs through our (IBM) practice of full employment."[10]

Another positive conclusion was reached by James F. Lincoln, former chairman of the highly successful Lincoln Electric Company, when he stated his case quite aptly in 1951. He said that "it is management's duty to make the worker secure in his job . . (so) that he can develop the skill and apply the imagination that will do his job more efficiently, without fear of unemployment from progress he makes."[11] Lincoln Electric continues to practice employment security today.

A number of studies have suggested the positive relationship between employment security and employee productivity. Others have completed research that are less conclusive in their findings. Leonard Greenhalgh states that "the evidence found in research literature to support this relationship is embryonic and mixed in its conclusions."[12] According to Richard E. Kopelman, Baruch College, The City University of New York, "there is a long history to the view that a lack of job security is an impediment to high productivity . . . (job security) does not assure high productivity: it may be a necessary condition but not a sufficient one."[13]

Although most of the literature focused on companies that practice employment security, there were few comparisons of practicing and non-practicing companies, or research that focused on companies that elected to discontinue the practice. The literature reviewed did not support the contention that employment security might have universal appeal; nor did it support the premise that if companies adopted the practice, advantages would offset disadvantages.

MEASUREMENT OF PRODUCTIVITY

In measuring productivity, the use of average annual dollar sales per employee is an accepted indicator, which is defined as outputs divided by inputs. While other measures of productivity might be used, this study used the output of goods and services sold in relation to resources consumed in producing these outputs. In one study of *Fortune* 500 companies completed by H. Edward Fenton, a marketing systems manager for *Reader's Digest*, it was determined that of the companies using productivity as a measurement, more than 50 percent used the number of employees as the measurement of input and more than 63 percent used total sales as the measurement of output. When measuring labor productivity, almost 50 percent of these same companies used sales per employee as the measurement.[14] This study will use average annual dollar sales per employee as the measure of productivity in comparing companies that practice employment security with those that do not, on an industry-by-industry basis. This same measure was used to compare the average annual increase in annual sales per employee for the years 1978–1987.

EXECUTIVE PERCEPTION AND EXPECTATIONS

The literature and statements from a number of researchers and business executives indicate that productivity should be more favorable for those companies that practice employment security. Much of the change accounted for in productivity is dependent on factors such as technological innovation, worker education and training, workforce restrictions, and job redesign. It has been suggested, however, that these factors are positively affected when employees are implicitly shown that increased productivity will not endanger their employment, even though their specific job assignment may change. The expectations are difficult to isolate and measure due to other factors that also impact employee productivity. The perception that the relationship between employment security and productivity exists may be non-existent, or at a minimum, not measurable.

As indicated, a number of studies have suggested the relationship. The expectation for this study is that there will be a significantly greater annual sales per employee for those companies that practice employment security. The annual rate of increase in sales per employee is also anticipated to be significantly greater for practicing companies, based on influences noted in studies cited.

SCOPE OF STUDY

The measurement of productivity of an organization is used to determine strategies, draw conclusions, seek trends, and finalize decisions. The productivity number, or change in that number, can indicate causal and subsequent problems that dramatically affect financial results.

Productivity is also used as a measurement of employee morale, employee trust in management, the result of technological change within the organization, the level of employee complacency, and the effectiveness of other internal or external operational changes. A relatively high level of productivity is necessary to assure success, and continued existence, of that organization. Productivity is also used as a national indicator of success and is called upon to measure national direction and global comparison.

As shown, annual sales per employee are commonly used as a measurement of productivity for a company or industry. This measurement was also used in this analysis in comparing, within each of thirteen industries (Table 4.2), those companies practicing employment security with those that do not, for the years 1978–1987. The level of significance was established at 0.05, and data was analyzed using t-tests for industry-to-industry comparisons and regression analysis for the year-to-year growth comparisons by industry.

Questionnaires were used to gather data from human resource executives of *Fortune* 500 companies, and *Fortune* was used for the sales data and number of employees. The questionnaires attained a 56 percent response: 65 percent from twenty-three companies practicing employment security and 51 percent from forty-one companies not practicing. Of the thirteen industries surveyed there was no response from two (chemicals and tobacco), three industries had responses from either the employment secure or the non–employment secure company, and the remaining eight industries had company responses from both groups. The questions asked sought to determine expectations from the human resource executives of whether an employment security practice would significantly affect the productivity of their firm.

FINDINGS—SALES PER EMPLOYEE

The survey responses received from the human resource executives indicated that they expected no significant difference between the two groups of companies. The expectation, when comparing annual sales per employee, was that employment security would significantly improve the rate of sales per employee when comparing companies within each of the industries.

The industry-by-industry analysis of annual sales per employee (Table 5.1) indicated no significant difference for four industries (aerospace, forest products, pharmaceutical, and to-bacco), which agreed with the human resource executives.

Table 5.1

Industry-by-Industry Analysis
Employment and Non–Employment Secure Company Data
Comparison of Annual Sales per Employee, 1978–1987

	Annual Sales t Value	Derived t Value
Aerospace	1.635	1.833
Chemicals	3.228	1.833
Computers	3.501	1.833
Electronics	10.091	1.833
Forest Products	1.224	1.943
Furniture	10.571	2.920
Metals	4.819	1.860
Motor Vehicles	8.980	1.833
Petroleum	27.234	1.833
Pharmaceutical	1.368	1.833
Scientific	3.167	1.833
Soap and Cosmetic	9.540	1.833
Tobacco	1.482	1.833

Note: Level of Significance = 0.05

Data: *Fortune* 500 annual listings.

Data comparisons for the remaining nine industries indi-cated that there is significant difference between those practicing employment security and those that do not. Further analysis of these nine industries show that sales per employee are significantly higher for those companies practicing employment security in five industries (electronics, furniture, metals, motor vehicles, and petroleum).

In the remaining four industries, those not practicing employment security reported significantly higher sales per employee (chemicals, computers, scientific and photographic, and soap). In three of these four industries the percentage change (using 1978 and 1987 year-end data) was greater companies practicing employment security. One industry (soap and cosmetic) was an exception, with both significantly higher annual sales per employee and a larger percentage change, comparing 1978 and 1987 data.

FINDINGS—YEAR-TO-YEAR CHANGE IN SALES PER EMPLOYEE

The annual rate of increase of sales per employee was expected to be significantly lower for those firms practicing employment security. This expectation was based on the premise that companies practicing employment security adjust manpower to changing economic conditions more cautiously that those companies not practicing.

Employees in the former category are treated as "quasifixed" expenses and are employed for the long term. Human resource plans and programs used by these companies to adjust employment levels do not include employee layoff. A more cautious approach is used for employee reduction and includes programs such as retirement incentive programs, voluntary employee buyout plans, reduced work hours, and reduced or no-hiring practices.

The implementation of programs such as these often results in a less dramatic change in employee population, as compared to the immediate reduction of personnel when a layoff is implemented. The programs utilized by those practicing employment security are said to be better accepted by employees; therefore, increased productivity is expected to support all or most of the change, and was expected to result in lower annual rate of change in sales per employee.

As sales increase, companies practicing employment security are said to act more conservatively in hiring practices, and often employ the use of workload buffers. These include the use of part-time and/or contract workers to help level the workload of full-time employees. Either situation was expected to result in a lower change in sales per employee for those practicing employment security.

Companies that do not practice employment security, on the other hand, are said to react to changing economic conditions and declining sales with immediate reduction of employees through layoff. When sales decline these abrupt changes in employment levels are expected to have a more significant impact on sales per employee. It is assumed that when sales increase these same companies will be more aggressive in their hiring practices because they do not have to manage the downside of declining workload or keep employees gainfully employed.

The human resource executives responding to the questionnaire reported that they expected no significant difference in rate of increase of sales per employee between the two groups.

CONCLUSIONS—ANALYSIS OF YEAR-TO-YEAR CHANGE

As shown in Table 5.2, the annual rate of change in sales per employee is significantly lower for companies practicing employment security in five of the thirteen industries (chemicals,

Table 5.2

Industry-by-Industry Analysis
Employment Secure and Non–Employment Secure
Annual Rate of Increase in Sales per Employee,1978–1987

	Rate of Increase t Value	Derived t Value
Aerospace	1.459	2.101
Chemicals	-3.152	2.101
Computers	-10.834	2.101
Electronics	-7.741	2.101
Forest Products	-1.611	2.179
Furniture	1.148	2.776
Metals	3.351	2.120
Motor Vehicles	10.283	2.101
Petroleum	10.788	2.101
Pharmaceutical	0.187	2.101
Scientific	-0.975	2.101
Soap and Cosmetic	-7.103	2.101
Tobacco	-3.784	2.101

Note: level of significance = 0.05

Data: *Fortune* 500 annual listings.

computers, electronics, soap and cosmetic, and tobacco products), a result in accord with expectations of the study. It was also determined that there is no significant difference in the annual rate of change for five industries (aerospace, forest products, furniture, pharmaceutical, and scientific and photographic). These industries experienced gradual change in sales, thus reducing the need for drastic action, such as employee layoff, to balance the workforce with sales.

The companies practicing employment security in the remaining three industries (metals, motor vehicles, and petroleum) reported a significantly higher rate of change. Of the latter three, the companies practicing employment security in the metals and motor vehicles industries also reported greater improvement in sales per employee when comparing year-end 1978 data with year-end 1987 data. In the petroleum industry, however, a lower percentage of improvement in sales per employee was reported by the employment secure company. Table 5.3 provides a summary of the two comparisons, sales per employee and annual rate of increase in sales per employee. The results, though inconclusive, indicate that productivity, as measured by sales per employee, is generally more favorable in companies that practice employment security.

IMPLICATIONS

This sector of the study found that on the average, productivity as measured by sales per employee was either not significantly different, or was significantly greater for nine of the thirteen industries reviewed. Analysis of the annual rate of change in sales per employee produced similar results, also somewhat mixed; with five industries showing no significant difference, five reporting a significant difference with the rate of change lower for those practicing employment security, and the remaining three industries reporting a significantly higher rate of change. The results generally lend support to the proponents of employment security.

The findings suggest that when firms provide employment security the productivity of that firm, as measured by sales per employee, will generally be more favorable. The implications are substantial for companies, government, and society due to the many problems resulting from large-scale layoffs.

Table 5.3

Employment Secure and Non–Employment Secure Comparison of Annual Sales per Employee and Rate of Change in Annual Sales per Employee, 1978–1987

| | Significant Difference in: | |
	Sales per Employee	Rate of Change
Aerospace	No	No
Chemicals	Yes (L)	Yes (L)
Computers	Yes (L)	Yes (L)
Electronics	Yes (H)	Yes (L)
Forest Products	No	No
Furniture	Yes (H)	No
Metals	Yes (H)	Yes (H)
Motor Vehicles	Yes (H)	Yes (H)
Petroleum	Yes (H)	Yes (H)
Pharmaceutical	No	No
Scientific	Yes (L)	No
Soap and Cosmetic	Yes (L)	Yes (L)
Tobacco	No	Yes (L)

Note: level of significance = 0.05

(L) = Significantly Lower
(H) = Significantly Higher

Data: *Fortune* 500 annual listings.

As mentioned previously, these findings need to be viewed with some caution. The data did not clearly demonstrate that a practice of employment security leads to, or brings about, higher or lower employee productivity. It is recognized that other variables have a bearing on productivity. While sales per employee are often used to measure productivity, productivity could have been assessed by other measures, raising the possibility that different results might have been attained. This analysis does, however, lead to some interesting discussions and thought processes from which strategies might be planned, pilot tests initiated, and conclusions drawn for a more universal acceptance or rejection of the premise that employment security does, or does not, affect the productivity of an organization.

NOTES

1.   Jenny Bortz, Audrey Brocker, Joel Brocker, Carolyn Carter, Jeanette Davy, and Jeff Greenberg, "Layoffs, Equity Theory, and Work Performance: Further Evidence of the Impact of Survivor Guilt," *Academy of Management Journal*, 1986, Vol. 29, No. 2, 373–384.

2.   Jerome M. Rosow and Robert Zager, *Employment Security in a Free Economy* (New York: Pergamon Press, 1984), 49.

3.   Paul Osterman, "Turnover, Employment Security and the Performance of the Firm," *Human Resources and the Performance of the Firm*, Industrial Relations Research Association, University of Wisconsin, 1987, 298–299.

4.   Ibid., 276–277.

5.   Marta Mooney, "Let's Use Job Security as a Productivity Builder," *Personnel Administrator*, January 1984, 39.

6.   Ibid., 38.

7.   Fred K. Foulkes and Anne Whitman, "Marketing Strategies to Maintain Full Employment," *Harvard Business Review*, July–August 1985, 30.

8.   James F. Bolt, "Job Security: Its Time Has Come," *Harvard Business Review*, November–December 1983, 116.

9. Results of a study conducted by Richard T. Pascale for the New York Stock Exchange. Cited in *People and Productivity: A Challenge to Corporate America*, New York Stock Exchange, 1984, 19–21.

10. James F. Bolt, "Job Security: Its Time Has Come," *Harvard Business Review*, November–December 1983, 116.

11. Mitchell Fein, "Motivation to Work," in *Handbook of Work, Organization and Society*, ed. Robert Dubin (Chicago: Rand-McNally, 1976), 512.

12. Leonard Greenhalgh, "Maintaining Organizational Effectiveness During Organizational Retrenchment," *Journal of Applied Behavioral Science*, 1982, 159.

13. Richard E. Kopelman, *Managing Productivity in Organizations* (New York: McGraw-Hill, 1986), 512.

14. H. Edward Fenton, "How Companies Use Productivity Measures," In Elliot S. Grossman, ed., *Productivity: The Challenge of the 1980s*, Conference Proceedings, Pace University, New York, 18 March 1983, 22–26.

6
Strategies and Results

Employment security has become a major goal of the organized and professional workforce in recent years. The U.S. corporate graveyard, however, is littered with bodies of companies that have won the battle of short-term "survival" but have lost the war in protection of employment for their employees. Social, business, and governmental trends toward protection of jobs have sputtered and stalled as a result of recession, changing job-skill requirements, global competition, and limited economic growth in a number of industries. These trends are forcing companies to rethink the strategic fundamentals of their business and determine the level of employment protection that is economically feasible. The public sector is also impacted by the sputtering economy and many of the same factors affecting employment in the private sector.

DECISION CRITERIA

As shown in Figure 6.1, a number of diverse and interlocking explicit and implicit forces influence decision criteria and determine levels of employment security.

Figure 6.1

Interacting Forces That Impact Employment Security Decisions in Organizations

Source: Paul H. Loseby, *A Review and Evaluation of Employment Security*, 1990, 18.

In recent times economic conditions and increased global competition are often the center of focus in the media, and are pressuring organizations to strive for excellence, survival, and "world class" status. This pressure is commonly accepted by U.S. corporate executives as a stimulus to business, emphasizing survival, continued financial profitability, and improvement of market share. Company executives find it necessary to identify and address each factor and challenge in the attempt to implement, contain, or continue the protection of employment for their employees.

Companies that offer employment security maintain the practice through effective management of their financial and operational priorities, and constant attention to factors that threaten workload imbalance. One common strategy used by many organizations to manage employment security is to use temporary, part-time, and contractual workers. These employees are often called contingent workers, or workers who are used as buffers to protect a core of permanent employees.

According to one study the number of contingent workers in the United States includes approximately 700,000 workers supplied by temporary-help agencies.[1] *The Wall Street Journal* estimates that when part-timers, self-employed contingent workers, contract workers, and consultants are included, the number approximates 34.2 million workers, or approximately one-third of the U.S. work force.[2] This use of contingent workers is often one of a number of strategies utilized. Other strategies used complement and interconnect with the use of temporary employees.

RECOMMENDED STRATEGIES

A number of successful strategies have been used to protect jobs, and the most meaningful and widely used are included in the policy recommendations discussed in the 1984 Work in America Institute (WIA) study (see Appendix I). These twenty-six recommendations address employment security strategies that protect all categories of employees. Each major strategy

group will be listed, along with examples showing application. The groupings are:
- Commitment to employment,
- Planning,
- Lean staffing,
- Short-term workload decline,
- Permanent workload decline,
- Alliances, and
- Government role.

THE COMMITMENT TO EMPLOYMENT

The first grouping of WIA recommendations address three basic stipulations to be met by employers. Commitment to employment by the firm is offered and legitimized explicitly with:

1. Commitment through an employer guarantee that permanent employees will not be laid off or downgraded due to labor surplus caused by internal productivity and/or performance changes. This commitment addresses and reduces the fear of job loss due to cooperative productivity and efficiency improvements between the employee and the firm.

2. Employers should issue the broadest affordable commitment to employment security that will be offered during times of business decline and address their intention of broader security coverage as business success increases. In addition, employers should promise an equitable distribution of sacrifice, if necessary.

3. Employers should make a written commitment to actively assist dismissed employees in seeking suitable jobs with other firms if that option is exercised.

APPLICATION OF COMMITMENT

A recent example of actions taken by Apple Computer, which strives to provide a level of security to its employees, took place in mid-1991. As a result of declining profits, Apple's executive management made the decision to eliminate 1,500 jobs. This would be accomplished through employee layoff over a twelve-month period with the primary emphasis on company survival and profitability. At the same time, Apple CEO John Sculley announced that he and other top executives would take pay cuts of up to 15 percent as a way to distribute the sacrifice and reduce the numbers laid off due to the trying times that Apple was faced with.[3] This example of management commitment and distribution of sacrifice exemplify the intent of the first three strategies noted.

PLANNING REQUIREMENTS

The study recommends strategies that stress the need for legitimate and continuing workload planning. This is noted as necessary and a "must" to be addressed by executive management of the firm. The study recommends that:

4. Human resource planning should become an integral part of the standard corporate business planning process.

5. All managers are deemed responsible for detailed human resource planning, with the primary responsibility fixed at the highest executive management level of the firm.

6. Challenges to employment security should be anticipated with plans in place to execute actions as required.

7. The CEO must have continual involvement and regular consultations with senior executives and international officers of the union to design and execute the best possible plan as required.

APPLICATION OF PLANNING

A number of planning strategies used by firms include operational and strategic plans to reduce or eliminate hiring for a period of time, redeployment of resources, training, and retraining. Some require action prior to layoff while others address actions that assist in employee readjustment to job market requirements. Examples of training and retraining to assist in readjustment of workforce to workload will be shown. The first, a program aimed at reemployment skill updating, resulted from negotiated agreement between the United Auto Workers (UAW) and Ford Motor Company. The provision was for a jointly operated UAW-Ford Employee Development and Training Program that is financially supported by a negotiated per-hour-worked contribution from the company. This program makes it possible for laid-off Ford employees to participate in training and gain marketable skills for reemployment. A second example of training in support of employment was instituted by the State of California. This program is funded by using a portion of tax paid by private-sector employees to support the federal/state unemployment insurance system. The separate fund for training and retraining is administered by the Employment Training Panel, drawn entirely from the private sector, and includes representatives from business and labor.[4]

Training and retraining have proven to be effective in providing job opportunity to those whose skills do not match the needs of the workforce. For example, of the 113,600 workers who participated in federally financed programs in 1984 and completed their training by June 1985, 65 percent had found jobs, according to a government study.[5]

A third example of planning takes place at Lincoln Electric Company. Every employee at Lincoln who has been on the payroll for two or more years is guaranteed employment of a least thirty hours a week, for forty-nine weeks each year. This "guarantee" has been sustained through the toughest of times for over fifty consecutive years (with the exception of layoffs required by the return to normal production at the end of World War II). One of Lincoln's strategies to fulfill this guarantee is through a tight control over hiring. This is an effective planning tool when anticipated workload and workforce can be projected. Every new hire must be approved by four vice presidents. Other companies practice a more common device of intentionally hiring fewer employees than are needed to handle normal market demand.

Planning as a strategy includes balancing workforce with anticipated workload and includes actions to reduce layoff, or at minimum provide options for new jobs or careers for those laid off.

MAINTAIN A LEAN ORGANIZATION

Other recommended strategies provide management focus on staffing and operating a lean organization. The following are suggested for action and consideration by management:

8. Management must resist accumulating surplus employees during prosperous times by ensuring that workforce levels are in synchronization with long-term workload needs;

assuring the competency of employees to meet changing needs; monitoring short-term increases of workload and managing these without adding protected employees; evaluating policies of major functional groups such as production, marketing, and finance to ascertain their commitment to employment security.

9. Staffing standards must be tough but realistic and adhere to basic premises such as: regard all new hires as career employees; make certain that protected employees are flexible and able to work effectively in a wide variety of assignments; address unsatisfactory performers expeditiously and early in their careers.

10. Workload buffers, when planned for and used, should assist in the maintenance of employment security and be used in accordance with published and agreed-upon ground rules to minimize any side effects on employee morale or company loyalty.

11. Firms seeking to stabilize work loads should focus on the stabilization of order flow, sustainable growth rates, diversity in markets served and customers marketed to, and flexibility in using production resources including people, plant, process, and materials.

APPLICATION OF LEAN STAFFING

To sustain lean staffing a number of organizations use overtime and temporary help to supplement the workload of non-exempt and paraprofessional workers. In professional areas, such as programming or engineering, the hiring of freelance professional contractors is common in protecting jobs of core workers. With large numbers of professional workers, vending and subcontracting of work are also used to avoid hiring of full-time employees. Xerox Corporation has at times filled the equivalent of 150 jobs through a contracting arrangement it calls "networking"; Hewlett-Packard also accounts for about that many jobs within its computer divisions through the hiring of freelance programmers, engineers, and technical writers. Another option, as used by IBM in some cases, is the recall of retired former employees.[6]

Control Data Corporation (CDC) also staffs for workload flexibility and hires additionally protected employees judiciously. CDC uses "buffer subcontracting," by contracting work to outside firms with the understanding that the work may be withdrawn during a business slump. This helps CDC avoid expansion of its permanent workforce more rapidly than its permanent workload warrants. At the same time CDC makes sure that permanent employees are trained to handle the work that may be pulled back in-house if conditions require.[7]

Motorola, in its semiconductor operation, staffs for 80 to 85 percent of normal demand. Prior to 1991, when IBM manufactured typewriters in Lexington, Kentucky, the giant operation was staffed to meet approximately 85 percent of normal demand. In both cases overtime, subcontract workers, part-time employees, or contract workers are used to meet the workload shortfalls.[8]

These examples of companies that offer some degree of employment security and actively practice lean staffing indicate that a number of formats can be successful. These strategies are planned and enforced within company culture, guidelines, and policy.

WORKLOAD DECLINES

Plans for short-term adversity and specific action required for economic decline, recessions, and/or product life-cycle decline, are necessary. A strategy response mechanism is recommended by WIA to include:

12. Restrictive hiring, returning vended work to be done in-house, expanding product or service demand, and assigning employees to lower-priority work as required.

13. When payroll costs must be reduced faster than restrictive hiring, all stakeholders in the firm should share equitably.

14. The employer should offer to employees faced with layoffs the alternative of remaining on the payroll and being paid the equivalent of unemployment benefits while taking part in education and training programs approved by the employer.

15. Prior to instituting layoffs, the employer should make it clear to employees and unions that there was no better solution.

APPLICATION OF SHORT-TERM ACTIONS

Short-term declines in workload can be managed a number of ways—from permanent layoff to redeployment and retraining. The latter mentioned options are more commonly used by companies protecting employment of their workforce. For example, Hallmark switches assignments to balance workload by assigning factory workers to maintenance and housekeeping jobs and by sometimes lending employees to the community. Other companies, such as IBM, Lincoln Electric, and Kimberly-Clark have followed the Japanese practice against short-term work decline by shifting factory, office, and staff personnel temporarily to sales-related positions.[9]

Another example of action taken to deal with short-term workload decline is a joint company/union venture, the UAW-Buick Employee Development Center. This program was established to address workload decline and is supported by a negotiated company contribution to a jointly managed fund and provides up to two years of retraining for Buick workers who will be displaced by the introduction of new technology, such as robots.[10]

One reason for the use of tactics shown is that layoffs can be costly and do not always provide the best solution to the financial crisis brought about by short-term market fluctuations. According to an analysis by Dan L. Ward in "The Cost Implications of a No-Layoff Policy," commissioned by the Work in America Institute, it was determined that the cost of removing 100 shop-floor employees at two manufacturing firms amounted to $741,500, or an average of $7,415 per employee. Thus the study concludes, "if an employer expects to need the same number of employees at the end of (temporary economic) decline as before, and expects the decline to last no longer than six months, then layoff and recall are probably more expensive, in strict bookkeeping terms, than retaining people on the payroll."[11]

PERMANENT WORKLOAD DECLINES

Suggested strategies that address permanent declines in workload are also required. This situation is often a more difficult predicament for executive management and could be managed by firms with the following strategies and actions:

16. Employers should make every effort to replace lost workload, reduce costs without dismissals, and help dismissed employees find suitable work.

17. Employers should retrieve work from temporary employees and contractors; then seek new products or services, acquire or create subsidiaries, or accept contracts from other firms.

18. If the permanent reduction of payroll costs is necessary, the employer should first use methods such as restrictive hiring, work sharing, phased retirement, wage reductions, and intensive productivity-raising programs.

19. If the dismissal of protected employees is unavoidable, the employer should help them find suitable work elsewhere, provide financial bridging, pension portability, outplacement services or retraining. The employer could also offer professional and financial assistance for those preferring self-employment. The employer could create or attract replacement jobs if the area suffers from a shortage of suitable jobs.

APPLICATION OF LONG-TERM ACTIONS

The United States can look to actions taken by Western European countries successful with job-replacement strategies in protecting their workers. In Western Europe this strategy involves using company funds as well as company expertise to help new enterprises get started or established in geographic locations affected by plant closures. The objective is to create new jobs and replace those lost by cutback or plant closure. The new jobs are not limited to the displaced workers but are also open to others in the community. This results in a "win-win" situation for the people and the community.

Another strategy used by Western European countries, and in the United States, to address long-term workload decline is the offering of an early retirement plan for older workers. This is an accepted and, it would appear, favorite buffering strategy to protect the employment security of the remaining workforce. In most Western European countries, laying off workers is not easy. Employers cannot adjust their workforce to changing economic conditions by laying off surplus workers at will, either temporarily or permanently. They must go through a series of mandatory, restrictive steps, which can include negotiations with the government as well as the union. Usually advance notice is required along with involvement with the state employment service industry, in addition to specified mandatory separation payments.

The French law stipulates that no one can be laid off for economic reasons without the specific permission of the state employment service. In West Germany, employers who wish to lay off personnel must prepare a "social plan" in cooperation with the union. This plan provides detail addressing the expected outcome for every laid-off worker and must be approved by the employment service agency. The British government is not as directly involved with layoffs as France or West Germany, but even in Great Britain advance notice of proposed layoffs is required, and specific separation payments are mandated.[12]

The strategy of early retirement of older workers is used extensively, and is generally accepted by U.S. workers. These early retirement packages are more prevalent among the professional white-collar workforce, while the blue-collar worker is often dealt with "the single most devastating blow to a person's psyche"—that of being laid off, according to Emily T. Smith, a writer for *Business Week*. In her article on stress she also mentioned problems that American workers have experienced with "early-out" retirement packages that are sometimes offered with conviction to older workers. One such fiftyish worker at General Motors was made an offer of early retirement, and weighed the option because "many of his colleagues had accepted similar offers. But four of them killed themselves shortly thereafter."[13] The change from employment to retirement can be dramatic even when financial packages are offered, but the strategy to provide financial assistance has been generally accepted in Europe and in the United States.

ALLIANCES

Another area addressed by the WIA study is the need for formation of alliances. This is viewed as important to sustain and solidify a practice of employment security and would include these actions:

20. Employers and local and international labor unions in a metropolitan area or major industrial region should form a computer-based job clearinghouse and keep it current.

21. Alliances should be formed by employers and unions to provide retraining and education for employees who have lost their jobs through no fault of their own.

22. Employers, local and international unions, and local and state governments should form alliances to diversify the job base in areas where there is a single industry or few firms.

USE OF ALLIANCES

The use of alliances to protect, or provide, employment opportunity are increasing, yet they are the exception. In the United States an alliance called the "Downriver Community Conference," a consortium of community-based agencies from sixteen local governments, is located "downriver from the Detroit area." This alliance has enjoyed success because of dynamic leadership and a dedicated and imaginative staff. The organization has moved from being a provider of government-funded training to being a community catalyst that brokers the development of new job-creating business, including defense contracts, for companies in the area.[14] This alliance of government, business, and community-based agencies has enjoyed positive results in placing the unemployed, and in the retention of jobs in the area.

Social institutions are also forming alliances and joining the numbers responding to the unemployed. In 1991 the rapid increase in the managerial unemployed in the northeast United States resulted in scores of churches forming small alliances with parishioners and counselors in support of unemployed members. A number of college business school placement offices are also supporting the unemployed by expanding their alliances to serve alumni as well as graduates.[15]

An example of an alliance that supports the unemployed overseas is found in a unique Swedish program, Landskrona Finans, which is jointly managed by a nationalized shipbuilding company, a union, and other employers in the area. These groups have joined together to capitalize and operate a development and finance agency and establish new businesses on the site of a shipyard being closed. Swedish national government support was also involved, since the shipyard was owned by Swedyard, the nationalized shipbuilding company. For the most part, the new venture is a private-sector initiative. The development and implementation of a plan prior to the closing of the shipyard enabled Landskrona Finans to maintain the level of economic activity, and replaced about a third of the lost jobs.[16]

GOVERNMENT'S ROLE

The employer, employee, unions, and other stakeholders need commitment and assistance from the government to successfully continue an employment security practice. Recommendations made by the Work in America Institute include the following:

23. Congress should establish a more rational balance between capital mobility and employment security by recognizing the rights of each citizen to tax protection against economic hardship, such as unemployment. Employers should be required to provide appropriately for employees who have been impacted as a result of a merger, acquisition, or leveraged buyout, and should be provided a tax write-off for keeping surplus employees on the payroll or helping them retrain or relocate to new jobs.

    Employees dismissed without fault should be allowed tax credits against future income, any decrease of earnings and benefits, and costs incurred in retraining for and relocating to a new job. Employer, employee, unions, and government should be in concert to deter unnecessary separations that benefit one party to the detriment to other stakeholders.

24. Recommendation that Short Time Compensation (STC) laws be passed in all states. This program is available in

seven states (California, Arizona, Oregon, Florida, Illinois, Washington, and Maryland) and is a government-authorized program whereby a firm may reduce the weekly hours worked by employees in order to spread the workload. The unemployment insurance system in these states would then compensate the affected workers.

25. Make STC payable to all otherwise eligible employees during unpaid hours for: voluntary on-the-job training, remedial education, skill development, or continuing education; supplementing partial wages of workers who perform work that is substantially less valuable than their normal work, or who are receiving outplacement assistance.

26. The federal government should assist employers who have given an explicit commitment of employment security against business declines. The assistance should consist of reimbursement for the net additional costs as a result of employee retention. This federal subsidy would require time and financial limits. However, the gross costs could be offset by savings in income-transfer and retraining programs, and by the continuation of tax revenues from employed workers.[17]

ACTION BY GOVERNMENT

The U.S. government has given little attention to policy directed toward controlling private industry's methods for workforce reductions. "This is despite the fact that layoff is the major cause of increases in unemployment," according to Dr. Harold Oaklander, professor of management at Pace University, New York.[18] Oaklander continues, "with free-flowing market characteristics of the United States economy in mind, advocates of full-employment have focused on the problems of the more vulnerable segments of the country's labor force, namely inexperienced youth, women, ethnic minorities with low work skills, and, to a lesser extent, the experienced but displaced elderly worker."

In the United States the decision to reduce a company's workforce remains at the discretion of the employer, just as it was 100 years ago. Progress has been made to protect jobs lost because of new technology—through legislation, and to a lessor extent through litigation. The overall effect to date has been a narrowing of the scope of "employment at will." Only a minority of state legislatures have adopted or considered laws that protect employment of people in the private sector.[19] The states of Maine and Wisconsin have, however, passed plant closing laws.

The Maine law applies to cases of voluntary closure or relocation of enterprises employing 100 or more workers. The Wisconsin law applies to cases of merger, liquidation, disposition, or relocation resulting in cessation of operations affecting an unspecified number of workers. Proposed legislation has also been submitted to the legislatures of a number of states (including Connecticut, Illinois, Maine, Massachusetts, Michigan, New Jersey, New York, Ohio, Oregon, Pennsylvania, and Rhode Island). It provides for one, or a combination of: advance notice, severance benefits, and community assistance fund contributions. It applies to the layoff of a given number or percentage of workers in an enterprise, or to plant closing or relocations affecting a given number or percentage of workers in an enterprise above a given size.

In cases involving a significant number of workers, advance notice is considered appropriate. If notice is not explicitly required by statute, U.S. courts are unlikely to read it into an employment contract. Few states have statutes requiring more than one week's advance notice. After a long and heated debate, the United States federal government in 1988 passed legislation requiring that large businesses give employees sixty days' advance notice of the intention to lay off a substantial portion of the workforce or close the plant.[20]

Practically no legislation exists at the national or state levels to restrict recourse to layoffs. However, in 1985 Massachusetts created an Industrial Services Program (ISP) to help shore up jobs in mature industries. The ISP helps potentially healthy companies get the capital they need to modernize equipment and prevent layoffs or shutdowns. The ISP does not normally invest in troubled businesses. Their focus is on making loans, in addition to acting as a consultant and unofficial broker, and assisting companies in obtaining financing from commercial sources. Results shown by ISP seem promising.[21]

Judicial and legislative law are slowly beginning to acknowledge that even employees who are not covered under union contract have an implicit employment commitment that cannot be severed at an employer's whim. However, changes in public policy toward a more humane job security arrangement are not coming from the federal government but from state laws and judicial interpretations. California is likely to pass the first law prohibiting unjust dismissal by private employers, and similar legislation is being proposed in four other states.

A New Jersey court recently forced Hoffman-LaRoche Inc. to uphold the job security assurances implied in its employee manual. In California, an appeals court prevented a discharge on the grounds that the employee was fired for declining to commit perjury; and in another case involving Atari Inc., a lawsuit was settled for more than $500,000 because the company had not warned 537 workers before dismissing them.[22]

In most Western European countries government plays a much more significant role in the conduct of business and employment practices than is the case in the United States. The government participation in Western Europe results in greater control and government involvement of employment practices. The arbitrary hiring and firing of employees is inhibited.

In Western Europe the government is also more involved in training and retraining. In France, employers are required to spend an amount equal to 1.5 percent of revenues for retraining. West Germany supports a substantial vocational education system and Sweden subsidizes employers who train workers who might otherwise be unemployed.[23]

While the reeducation of workers plays a big role, the countries in Western Europe are committed to full employment of their citizenry. In West Germany a top priority for the government is keeping people employed. Proposals to move a plant, for example, are subjected to close scrutiny by the government. If work tapers off, employees are put on "short-time working" and the government pays the difference to keep employees at full wages.

Under the Protection Against Dismissal Act, an employer who has dismissed a significant number of employees (as defined by the law) has the burden of proving that none of these was the victim of a "socially unwarranted dismissal." This is defined as a dismissal "not based on reasons connected with the person or conduct of the worker, or on urgent operating requirements precluding his continued employment in the undertaking." Courts have held that a fall in profits is not *per se* an "urgent operating requirement." Advance notice of up to three months must be provided to the employee, and to the works council. This has resulted in 20 percent of layoffs being averted, and more than half of another 10 percent winning compensation before a labor court.[24]

This more active role by government in Western Europe explains some of the difference in reported unemployment rates. It also may explain some of the interest in the formation of alliances that address and counteract loss of employment. Except for the plant closing notice requirement enacted in 1988, there is little in United States legislation that compares with the well-established statutory protection abroad.

In the public sector, the U.S. Supreme Court has tended to favor job security for public employees. The court has ruled that workers have rights to liberty and property under the Fourteenth Amendment, and even authorized a tort of wrongful discharge in cases in which filing for workers' compensation triggers the discharge.

KEYS TO SUCCESS

One of the keys to the success of employment security requires the effective execution of well-planned strategies, in addition to commitment and action by the key stakeholders in the process; employers, employees, unions, and the government. It is important that stockholders and financial investors buy into the process, but it is imperative that the employer, employee, unions, and government all understand that they must exemplify the strongest commitment and each must completely accept their responsibilities. The Work in America Institute study identified key areas and strategies required to address the business challenges resulting from changes in sales and workload.

EMPLOYER

The employer faces an enormous challenge in times of economic adversity and declining workload. Management commitment and the need for strategies are necessary prior to reaching times of crisis. Past experience has indicated that when economic times are positive the development of action plans for declines in business is often ignored. In America the focus, or planning, for bad times during times of economic growth is often seen as counterproductive and negative. Management energy is more often devoted to positive outlook, such as growth and improvement of product lines. This pushes business planning for increased market share and profit dollars while presenting a more optimistic focus for management. The "what-if" plans are, therefore, often set aside until the crisis is at hand. The often-repeated quote, "don't wait to drain the swamp until waist deep in alligators" applies.

Another factor mentioned is that "lean measures" are necessary. This is counter to the way many U.S. businesses are managed. When economic times are on the upswing, controllable expenses such as travel, recognition events, or additions to staff are often accepted as perks as a result of success, a positive business outlook, and prosperity. Employee hiring cycles often follow the business cycle. When sales are increasing so also do support staff and direct employee population. When the business cycle declines, staff is reduced and promises are made within the management ranks that more control will be placed on staff growth once the cycle bottoms out.

EMPLOYEE

The employee also has definite responsibilities that must be accepted in order for employment security to be effective.

Some of these responsibilities are difficult to accept by employees when the business cycle dictates that all levels of staff in an organization must share in adversity. The employee must remain flexible in type of work performed, physical location worked at, training/retraining programs necessary, education programs required, career changes necessary, and sometimes even reversal to a position that he or she had been promoted from some time earlier. For example, during a recent business downturn one company practicing employment security asked former salespeople, who had achieved higher-level staff positions, to return to selling.

In addition the employee may be asked to work reduced hours or to accept salary decreases. When faced with the alternative between layoff and one or more of these options the potential financial burden on the employee appears low, with acceptance high. The employee's positive acceptance of these actions is critical. Many of these affect egos and personal goals, yet may offer a more acceptable alternative than job loss, even when required for a relatively long period of time.

GOVERNMENT

The government role, as recommended by the Work in America study, appears to have the greatest distance to travel in order to come into synchronization with employer and employee requirements and strategies. Federal legislation that addresses the issues and assists the other stakeholders has been slow in the proposal and enactment stages. The political atmosphere is affected by the economy and the particular "hot" button at the time. When the national economy is prosperous the focus of Congress is often on issues of the day, not usually on employment security. At the other extreme, when the economy turns downward and the business and workload decline is in motion, government focus is on money-saving measures and protection of the tax base. Legislative action that is necessary to save peoples' jobs is often not given the priority that it deserves. It is a "catch-22" situation.

UNIONS

The unions have provided much focus in recent years on the importance of employment security. They have made a number of concessions to management in the effort to save jobs and have been relatively successful. Cooperation and collaboration with former adversaries has made progress and must continue.

ALLIANCES

The formation of alliances among the key stakeholders is also necessary. This is a positive move that companies, unions, and employees could form at any time. Again, the focus and energy are often not applied until the crisis is present. This move is accepted and is being taken in some areas of the United States to provide active job banks funded by joint venture of the groups. Future studies will confirm the adequacy and success of these joint efforts.

SUMMARY

The key to the successful implementation of strategies is that the responsibilities of an employment security practice must be shared by all groups: employers, employees, unions, and the government. The strategies must also be explicitly supported by the stockholders and other financial investors. A long-term commitment must be made by all stakeholders, rather than basing decisions on quarterly statements.

These issues were effectively stated by Tom Peters in *Thriving on Chaos*, when he concluded that employment security involves three major issues:

1. providing security in return for flexibility and risk taking on everyone's part,
2. treating the workforce as a long-term "asset" worthy of constant reinvestment (e.g., retraining), and
3. shifting from a mindset that sees cost reduction as a primary goal (with labor a "factor of production") to a revenue enhancement strategy.[25]

NOTES

1. Audrey Freedman, "Perspectives on Employment," *The Conference Board*, Research Bulletin #114, 1986, 13.

2. Michael J. McCarthy, "Managers Face Dilemma With Temps," *The Wall Street Journal*, 5 April 1988, 39.

3. Laurie Kretchmar, "Biting Apple," *Fortune*, July 29, 1991, 43.

4. Jocelyn F. Gutchess, *Employment Security in Action: Strategies That Work* (New York: Pergamon Press, 1985), 7.

5. Jacob Schlesinger and Melinda Grenier Guiles, "Struggling Back," *The Wall Street Journal*, 16 January 1987, 13.

6. Joseph A. Raelin, "Job Security for Professionals," *Personnel*, July 1987, 43.

7. Chris Lee, "The Argument for Employment Security," *Training*, April 1985, 10–11.

8. Tom Peters, *Thriving on Chaos* (New York: Harper and Row, 1988), 419.

9. Ibid., 419.

10. Jocelyn F. Gutchess, *Employment Security in Action: Strategies That Work* (New York: Pergamon Press, 1985), 8.

11. Chris Lee, "The Argument for Employment Security," *Training*, April 1985, 11.

12. Jocelyn F. Gutchess, *Employment Security in Action: Strategies That Work* (New York: Pergamon Press, 1985), 73.

13. Emily T. Smith, "Stress: The Test Americans are Failing," *Business Week*, 18 pril 1988, 74.

14. Jocelyn F. Gutchess, *Employment Security in Action: Strategies That Work* (New York: Pergamon Press, 1985), 10.

15. Patricia A. Langan, "The New Executive—Unemployed," *Fortune*, 8 April 1991, 42.

16. Jocelyn F. Gutchess, *Employment Security in Action: Strategies That Work* (New York: Pergamon Press, 1985), 10.

17. Jerome M. Rosow and Robert Zager, *Employment Security in a Free Economy* (New York: Pergamon Press, 1984), 4–13.

18. Harold Oaklander, "Workforce Reductions in Undertakings—U.S. Report," *The Center for Applied Research*, Pace University, The Lubin School of Management, New York, May 1982, 188.

19. Edmund F. Byrne, *Work, Incorporated* (Philadelphia: Temple University Press, 1990), 170–171.

20. Ibid., 169.

21. John E. Schwarz and Thomas J. Volgy, "Experiments in Employment—A British Cure," *Harvard Business Review*, March–April 1988, 108.

22. Joseph A. Raelin, "Job Security for Professionals," *Personnel*, July 1987, 41.

23. Jocelyn F. Gutchess, *Employment Security in Action: Strategies that Work* (New York: Pergamon Press, 1985), 11.

24. Edmund F. Byrne, *Work, Incorporated* (Philadelphia: Temple University Press, 1990), 169–170.

25. Tom Peters, *Thriving on Chaos* (New York: Harper & Row, 1988), 422.

7
Challenge of Application

The Work in America Institute recommended strategies that capture the essence of strategic alternatives, employment commitment, and government policies required to provide employment protection in the United States. Permanent operating strategies are identified and depicted in Figure 7.1. These are necessary for management of employment security, adjustment to temporary economic cycles, and permanent planning for declines in job-skill requirements. Actions taken and strategies implemented are discussed in the following examples.

It has been implied that a strategy, or combination of strategies, must be planned and implemented to successfully protect jobs. The application of these strategies sometimes provides unexpected results—generally due to the management process rather than to the use of a specific strategy. For example, the use of temporary help for peak workload demands is used successfully by many companies, and presents problems to others. An example of the latter was noted in *The Wall Street Journal*.

Figure 7.1

How to Manage Employment Security

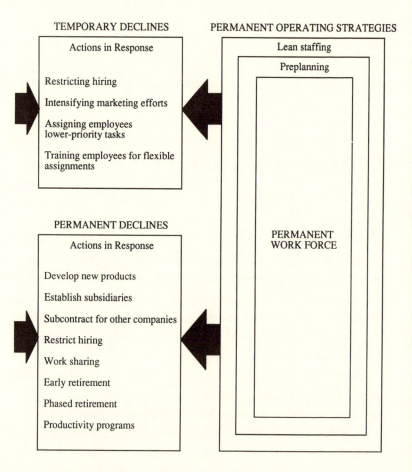

TEMPORARY DECLINES

Actions in Response

Restricting hiring

Intensifying marketing efforts

Assigning employees
lower-priority tasks

Training employees for flexible
assignments

PERMANENT OPERATING STRATEGIES

Lean staffing

Preplanning

PERMANENT
WORK FORCE

PERMANENT DECLINES

Actions in Response

Develop new products

Establish subsidiaries

Subcontract for other companies

Restrict hiring

Work sharing

Early retirement

Phased retirement

Productivity programs

Source: Jerome M. Rosow and Robert Zager, *Employment Security in a Free Economy*, 1984m, 14-15.
Reprinted by permission of Work in America Institute, Inc.

The situation occurred shortly after a company (Corroon and Black Corporation) hired a temporary worker to stuff 80,000 insurance certificates into envelopes. Upon "completion" of this task the company found thousands of the documents dumped into a freight elevator. Upon investigation by management it was determined that the "temp" had become bored working alone and thought nobody would notice if she cut her workload.[1] Since that finding, changes have been made at Corroon and Black Corporation to provide additional training for and attention to their temporaries. The company also now provides name plates, restroom keys, and internal memos related to their work, and when feasible the temporary employees work together on projects.

Other companies call on different strategies to manage peak workload situations, as well as workload decreases. One such company that has been successful at managing employment security for the long term is Lincoln Electric, the world's largest manufacturer of arc-welding machines and electrodes. Their basic strategy for handling a drop in workload decline is to reduce hours worked and bonus payments. In 1982, when Lincoln's company sales plummeted 40 percent, workers' hours were reduced and bonus payments dropped from $59 million paid in 1981 to $26.5 million in 1983. The strategy to initiate a flexible workweek paid off for Lincoln and without the flexible-bonus plan, "we couldn't have maintained guaranteed employment," says Richard Sabo, assistant to the chief executive officer.[2]

Materials Research Corporation (MRC), another company that has been successful in maintaining employment security, had initiated a formal policy but had not identified strategies to handle workload decreases when the 1981 recession hit. As business slowed, the company determined that they had 100 surplus tool workers. MRC quickly implemented strategies that included a halt to the hiring process and finding work for surplus employees. A job rotation program was also started and employees were temporarily assigned to other jobs for short periods of time. In addition, task groups were formed to identify work that had been previously been put on hold due to more urgent tasks. MRC also implemented employee education programs.

Each strategy played a role in the success of remaining a viable business while not laying off employees. In the 1982-1983 recession MRC spent an estimated $4 million in pay and benefits for surplus employees. This equates to money that would have increased the company's pre-tax earnings at least fourfold. According to management at MRC, two clear benefits realized as a result of protecting employee jobs were: recruitment and hiring were easier due to the company's positive public image, and employee attitudes and company loyalty were invaluable to the company.[3]

PUBLISHED STUDIES

The Conference Board completed a study following a recent recession in an attempt to determine cost-reduction methods used by organizations. It was found that more than three-fifths of the 171 large industrial companies surveyed reported making significant cutbacks in personnel as one of the primary methods used to reduce costs. The cutbacks ranged from hiring freezes to permanent separations, and varied appreciably by industry and type of employee. This sample of *Fortune* 500 industrial companies indicated that 105 companies made significant reductions in at least one category of worker (unionized blue-collar, non-union blue-collar, office, technical, or managerial).[4]

David Hershfield, who works in management research for *The Conference Board*, writes that the majority of companies manage personnel reductions by not filling vacancies caused by normal attrition. According to Hershfield, this is the accepted practice for white-collar workers; for blue-collar workers greater reliance is placed on layoffs. Temporary layoffs (defined as those that include a possibility of recall) are shown to be the most common method utilized when downsizing the number of unionized blue-collar workers, and were used in 87 percent of reported cases. By contrast, when layoffs do occur for white-collar workers, permanent separations rather than temporary layoffs are used more frequently.[5]

A survey of 1,005 corporations conducted jointly by 5 and the Wyatt Company consulting firm in early 1991 found that 86 percent of the companies surveyed had reduced their managerial ranks in the prior five years, and 52 percent of them had done so in 1990. Managerial downsizing has taken even deeper hold in companies with more than 5,000 employees—90 percent of these had slashed their white-collar payroll over the prior five years; 59 percent in 1990. Probably even more noteworthy, 41 percent of the top human resource executives polled say that the ranks of managers are likely to experience additional shrinkage in the next five years. Only 25 percent expect the numbers to grow.[6] With the number of executive and white-collar jobs on the wane, laid-off executives are often without jobs for eight months or more according to Drake Beam Morin, the nation's largest outplacement firm. This is two months longer than it took this same group of people to find new positions in 1989.

In the 1990–1991 recession managers and professionals experienced the biggest share of layoffs at the start of the recession. In August 1990, for example, white-collar layoffs accounted for 67 percent of the increase in joblessness from the year before. By November, blue-collar workers accounted for 72 percent of the increase in unemployment over the previous year.

The importance of a hiring control strategy is shown in another study. Managers of six companies successful in avoiding layoffs during the recession of the 1970's were studied. These companies included Bell Laboratories, Mallinckrodt, 3M Company, Polaroid, Texaco, and Wyeth Laboratories. The study showed that the approaches used to eliminate layoffs were standard for most—establish a policy not to have layoffs, and institute management practices to carry out that policy.[7] The study concluded that hiring controls are a crucial factor in limiting the accumulation of large staffs during favorable business cycles.

WRITTEN COMMITMENT

Although a number of companies practice employment security, few have committed to the practice in writing. The reasons for this reluctance range from legal liability to executive management's uncertainty about maintaining the practice over time. Material Research Corporation (MRC) is one company that has provided a written commitment to their employees. MRC has maintained an impressive track record of not laying off employees for more than 25 years. The existence of the program goes deeper than humanitarian concerns, according to Sheldon Weinig, chairman of MRC. Mr. Weinig has stated that, "although I believe employees have to be treated humanely, there is a primary business reason. It's just good management of the company's assets."[8] The assets referred to are key to the success of any company, yet the tangible costs of maintaining employment security is often easier to measure than tangible benefits.

The benefits realized by MRC, as noted previously, include conservation of recruitment and training resources. MRC also realized an increase in "productivity, employee motivation, morale, loyalty and commitment to the company. Furthermore, employees' efficiency has been increased by reducing their anxiety during business crises."[9]

The 1984 Work in America Institute study (Table 7.1), proposed staffing strategies necessary to maintain employment security. The establishment of goals and objectives, hiring controls, and executive support and direction are all deemed necessary.

Table 7.1

How to Manage Employment Security: Staffing Strategies

When companies seek employment security for their employees, they plan for adverse business conditions but keep their workforce lean the year round by:

1. Matching workforce levels to long-term demand

2. Hiring employees with special attention to competence

3. Encouraging flexibility by training employees to fill a variety of jobs

4. Appraising employee performance frequently and taking appropriate action

5. Meeting temporary workload increases without adding permanent employees by using:
    a. overtime
    b. temporary employees
    c. subcontracting
    d. transfer of employees from units with smaller workloads

6. Stabilizing demand

7. Using flexible production methods

Source: *Employment Security in a Free Economy*, 1984, 79.

ADDITIONAL APPROACHES

Strategies used by U.S. companies include innovative approaches to retraining employees for changing labor skills required in the current labor market. An example of this approach includes a program developed jointly by the Buick Division of General Motors and the United Auto Workers. This program provides employees who are scheduled to be displaced with up to two years of full pay and benefits while workers retrain and prepare themselves for other jobs or new careers.

Another approach, instituted by the Amalgamated Clothing and Textile Workers Union, includes a plan for union membership to assist in the development of new technology, thus enabling the industry to better compete with foreign exports (and imports) and thus save American jobs.[10]

MANAGEMENT OPPORTUNITIES

Historical results from the ineffective use of strategies shown in Figure 7.1 and Table 7.1 have been apparent. Layoffs and dismissals of employees in the United States have been standard responses to challenging times; resolving short-term deficiencies as well as long-term dilemmas, and in adjusting to business downturns and to the reality of longer-term recessions. These adjustments to personnel have been used since the great industrial revolution of the late 1800's. Recent data indicate that in manufacturing, where layoffs most frequently occur, the rate of layoffs per year for the years 1968–1981 fluctuated between 0.9 percent and 2.1 percent, with the mean duration of time ranging between 6.8 weeks and 14.5 weeks.[11]

Published statistics often provide measurable, global data on the percentage of unemployed workers, or length of time out of work, without addressing the social and human effects of layoff. Layoff is said to be the single most devastating blow to a person's psyche. This can be shown best by reviewing the result of layoffs of 6,800 employees since 1984 at the Phillips Petroleum Company. These results have had far-reaching effects in the Bartlesville, Oklahoma, company headquarters. Statistics from 1987 were gathered from Women and Children in Crisis, a local shelter and counseling center for abused families. These data tell a grim tale: requests for assistance increased 69 percent, women attending support groups for battered wives increased 41 percent, and the number of women in counseling groups rose 74 percent.[12]

CRITICAL FACTORS

It has been suggested by a number of writers that certain identifiable factors are critical to the success of employment security. Executive direction and management commitment are two of these. Based on literature it appears that a number of companies instituted their employment practice at the time the company was founded, or when the firm underwent a major restructuring process. The practice was often the result of the belief system and philosophy of the entrepreneurial founder. One such success story that exemplifies these premises and commitments can be found in the ideals of the largest and most successful computer company in the world, International Business Machines Corporation (IBM).

EMPLOYMENT SECURITY AS PRACTICED BY IBM

The success of an employment security practice can be measured by the longevity of the practice, the number of firms practicing, and the effort put forth by companies to prolong the practice. In some instances the obstacle of too little workload with too many people cannot be overcome using strategies listed. Even in those cases where workforce reduction by layoff is necessary for long-term survival, success can be measured by intent and management effort to prevent layoff or to place employees in meaningful jobs after layoff.

Companies that have managed to overcome adversity caused by recessions, technological change, or market change and maintain employment security are few. IBM, the most profitable company in the world, is one such company, and is one of the most challenged companies in the 1990's due to technological change, global competition, and a shifting market. IBM has introduced programs to reduce employees on a voluntary basis since the mid-1980's. In 1991 IBM announced another voluntary employee retirement option, hoping to reduce its employee headcount by 20,000 additional people.

IBM'S BASIC BELIEF

Since the founding of IBM in 1914 the message and commitment of Thomas J. Watson, Sr., has prevailed. Watson committed the IBM company to three basic beliefs, one of which is the company's implicit and explicit dedication to practice and support "respect for the individual." This basic belief has been interpreted by IBM employees to mean a number of things: from providing each employee with the capability to openly and directly communicate with the chairman of the board on issues and concerns, to the practice positively accepted by IBM employees for more than fifty years, employment security for those who are performing their jobs in a satisfactory manner. The practice does not guarantee that an employee, for the term of his IBM employment, will be working on the same job or within the same avocation. The practice does infer, however, that an employee will be given the opportunity to train or retrain for another position or avocation when and if the present job is eliminated due to technological change, economic conditions, or for other reasons.

STRATEGIES UTILIZED BY IBM

An example of measures taken to protect jobs at IBM was recently addressed by John F. Akers, IBM chairman of the board. Mr. Akers, as speaker at the Detroit Economic Club, relayed that "the IBM company is going through one of the most abrupt and rapid transformations in its history," and has initiated the following actions in order to sustain its employment security practice:

- The company has reduced costs and expenses by moving people to work and work to people, within the confines of the company.
- Plant sites have been closed and remissioned with all affected employees offered jobs and reassigned to other areas.
- Staff functions (positions) have been reduced significantly.
- Voluntary retirement incentives were offered to reduce the employee population.[13]

Employment security has prevailed at IBM because of actions such as these. The employee decision of whether to remain with IBM continues to be personal and voluntary, even with mission changes and retirement incentive options. In 1986 IBM completed the biggest restructuring in its history—and one of the largest retraining and relocation efforts ever undertaken by a company. IBM moved more than 15,000 of its 237,000 U.S. employees into new jobs, with an additional 13,000 electing early retirement with financial incentives. At one plant closing, more than 500 employees moved to other IBM jobs, 400 retired with up to two years' pay added to augmented pension plans, and 44 workers left the company after being offered positions elsewhere.[14]

ACTIONS TAKEN BY IBM

IBM has a list of strategies that are activated to preserve employment security during the difficult times. The action taken does not always follow the sequence shown below, and "so far it's avoided the last three measures, which would be most disruptive to its workers."[15] They are:

1. Constantly retrains workforce, and moves work between IBM plants.
2. Reduces temporary work and overtime.
3. Has employees take unused vacations and encourages leaves of absence.
4. Limits student internships in laboratories and other facilities.
5. Limits employee requests to transfer to overstaffed plants.
6. Curtails or freezes hiring.
7. Asks workers to move voluntarily to other IBM facilities.

8. Requests workers returning from leave to go to other plants or locations.
9. Sets up voluntary early retirement incentives.
10. Brings work back to IBM plants that has been contracted out.
11. Has other IBM plants hire workers away from overstaffed plants (locations).
12. Transfers employees to other comparable jobs in the same plant.
13. Transfers workers to lower-grade jobs.
14. Relocates employees to positions at other IBM plants.[16]

As John F. Akers told stockholders at the IBM annual stockholder meeting in April 1987, "with all these actions, our historic practice of full employment has been preserved . . . one of the important platforms not only for IBM's past and future success, but also for the well-being of our people. Morale throughout the business remains high."[17]

SIGNIFICANT RETRAINING OF IBM EMPLOYEES

The retraining of employees in IBM has always been of great importance in sustaining employment security. In 1984 IBM retrained 5,000 of its 23,000 U.S. employees for new jobs because "skills and resource needs changed significantly," according to Walton F. Burdick, IBM personnel vice president.[18] In 1986 consolidations and the thrust for leaner staffs stimulated the move of 2,500 people from marketing staffs to the field (marketing positions as salespeople and systems engineers). Another 4,000 people from manufacturing plants and laboratories also were also assigned to the field as sales representatives, marketing support, customer engineers, etc. This massive re-training effort again emphasized IBM's commitment to employment security. Says Burdick: "people have to be willing to be retrained. And reassigned. And redeployed. And in some instances, though not all, relocated."[19]

The expense involved in retraining, relocating, and redeploying employees is sizable. In 1985 IBM spent $550 million educating workers—from training secretaries to be technicians, to teaching engineers how to keep pace in a rapidly changing profession. In all, some 10,000 employees were trained for new jobs, with 7,300 changing locations at an estimated cost of $50,000 to $60,000 for each relocation. Nearly half of these relocations were for workload balancing; the remainder were promotions or for other reasons.[20]

IBM does not provide an ironclad promise of a lifetime job to their employees. The employees, however, do recognize the mutual commitment and accepted philosophy of "respect for the individual" as a tradition that is voiced and explicitly committed to by management. When employees were asked, "how satisfied are you that you will be able to work for IBM as long as you perform satisfactory work?" a high percentage responded saying they were "very satisfied" or "satisfied" that their jobs were secure.

Employment security continues to remain a "valued—and valuable—tradition" with IBM employees. This is indicated in employee response to surveys completed by IBM employees and compared to employees of other companies when asked to rate their company on employment security. Over a six-year period from 1981–1986, IBM employees consistently provided a high favorable response, while employees of other companies responded more than 30 percent lower. According to Walton Burdick the importance of employment security is a major factor in shaping employee views of a company. "While other companies responded to industry slowdowns with layoffs—and so were able to improve short-term financial results quickly—IBM continued its no-layoff practice. I think we'll (IBM) reap long-term benefits through our most important asset—people."[21]

RESULTS AND EXPECTATIONS

Findings shown from studies are inconclusive. It does, however, appear that the claims of critics—or claims of writers who support employment security because of increased productivity, improved employee morale, or improved company loyalty—are unfounded. One may continue to ask why management should expend resources to support and manage employment security when so few benefits are substantiated.

As is the case with a number of other business policies and practices, the position taken by entrepreneurs, company presidents, and executive management is sometimes based on intuition, social and ethical beliefs, and subjective data rather than on substantiated facts. Employment security appears to be one such policy or practice that is a part of the intuitive belief system possessed and practiced by some U.S. business leaders.

Employment security practices have been in existence and maintained by companies for a number of years; through recessions, depressions, and cyclical changes of less magnitude. Some companies have employed the practice for more than fifty years and although threatened at times, management commitment and long-term practices provided necessary focus and continuance during these business down-cycles.

Employment security presents a number of management challenges as shown: training and retraining of personnel, establishment of employee transition programs to meet changing business needs, and regular assessment of workload requirements matched to skill-mix availability.

When reviewing the list of companies that practice or have practiced employment security, the declining number of participants suggests that companies often abandon these practices at times of financial difficulty, while those that do not subscribe to the practice seldom institute the practice when financial conditions are relatively favorable. Many companies that maintain employment security continue to cite intangible benefits such as improved employee morale, increased company loyalty, and better employee productivity over the long term. These benefits may indeed exist and these companies may have evidence demonstrating the benefits. One commonality among all active participants is management commitment and the active use of some or all of the strategic options shown in Figure 7.1 and Table 7.1.

SUMMARY

The haunting question that remains following research and analysis of those practicing employment security and those that have discontinued the practice in times of adversity is, "why have some been successful while others failed?" For example, Digital Equipment Corporation practiced employment security for thirty-four years and utilized many of the strategies recommended. It also had the management commitment as voiced by Ken Olsen, DEC's president. What happened to it and large corporations such as Intel, Eastman Kodak, and others? Did the projected expense exceed the perceived benefits? Did management give up too quickly? Were morale, productivity, and loyalty affected by the layoffs at those companies? These and many more unanswered questions remain. The only known fact is that a few major U.S. corporations are dedicated to employment security and do in fact utilize many of the strategies advocated in order to retain the practice and remain profitable while doing so. The recession of the early 1990's, combined with other factors, has challenged the most committed employment security practices in the United States, even IBM's.

NOTES

1. Michael J. McCarthy, "Managers Face Dilemma with Temp," *The Wall Street Journal*, 5 April 1988, 39.

2. Alan Murray, "Why Unions Like Fixed Pay," *The Wall Street Journal*, 28 April 1987.

3. Jocelyn F. Gutchess, *Employment Security in Action: Strategies That Work* (New York: Pergamon Press, 1985), 20–23.

4. David C. Hershfield, "Reducing Personnel Costs During Recession," *Conference Board Record*, June 1975, 20.

5. Ibid., 22.

6. Patricia A. Langan, "The New Executive: Unemployed," *Fortune*, 8 April 1991, 37.

7. Howard J. Sanders, "Employees Tell How To Avoid Layoffs," *Chemical Engineering News*, 3 December 1973, 13.

8. Sheldon Weinig, Guaranteed Lifetime Employment Pays Off Employee Commitment," *AMA Forum*, August 1984, 35.

9. Ibid.

10. Jocelyn F. Gutchess, "Employment Security Strategies," *Worklife*, Canada, 1985, 9.

11. Jerome M. Rosow and Robert Zager, "The Case For Employment Security," *Across The Board*, January 1985, 38.

12. Emily T. Smith, "Stress: The Test Americans are Failing," *Business Week*, 18 April 1988, 74.

13. John F. Akers, speech on American competitiveness, presented to the Detroit Economic Club, 11 February 1987.

14. Dennis Kneale, "Tough Choices," *The Wall Street Journal*, 8 April 1987, 1.

15. Aaron Bernstein, "IBM's Fancy Footwork to Sidestep Lay-offs," *Business Week*, 7 July 1986, 5.

16. Ibid.

17. John F. Akers, speech presented at the IBM stockholders' meeting, New Orleans, 27 April 1987.

18. Richard Brandt, "Those Vanishing High-Tech Jobs," *Business Week*, 15 July 1985, 31.

19. Carol J. Loomis, "IBM's Big Blues: A Legend Tries To Remake Itself," *Fortune*, 19 January 1987, 52.

20. Aaron Bernstein, "IBM's Fancy Footwork to Sidestep Lay-offs," *Business Week*, 7 July 1986, 54–55.

21. "Maintaining a Valued and Valuable Tradition," *IBM Management Report*, Armonk N.Y., September 1987, 10.

8
Managing in the 21st Century

Since the start of modern business enterprise, after the Civil War in the United States, there have been major evolutions in concept and structure of organizations. According to Peter Drucker, a widely known author and scholar on management processes and thought, the first evolution took place between 1895 and 1905. It distinguished management from ownership and clearly established management as work and task in its own right. Examples of this evolutionary change can be viewed in the massive restructuring of U.S. railroads and major industries by well-known business leaders such as J. P. Morgan, Andrew Carnegie, and John D. Rockefeller, Sr.

The second major change took place some twenty years later. The development of the modern corporation began with Pierre S. Du Pont's restructuring of his family controlled company in the early 1920's and continued with Alfred P. Sloan's redesign of General Motors a few years later. This change introduced the command-and-control organization of today, with emphasis on decentralization, central staff functions, personnel management, budget, and controls, and distinction between line and staff. This stage reached its peak in the early 1950's when General Electric instituted massive reorganizations. This model is followed by most big businesses around the world today.

According to Drucker we are now entering a third period of change: the shift from command-and-control, with its departments and divisions, to the information-based organization, the organization of knowledge specialists. Though the elements and structure of this 20th-century structure are slowly evolving, the challenge to be faced include thè actual building of this information-based organization, while protecting demographic change and anticipating supply and demand of labor.

EVOLVING ORGANIZATION OF THE 21st CENTURY

The change is underway, according to Drucker, and can be recognized in pharmaceuticals, telecommunications, electronics, and other industries. The traditional sequence of research, development, manufacturing, and marketing is being replaced by a "synchrony": specialists from each of these functions working together as a team from inception of a product to establishment of that product in the market.[1]

As in any evolutionary process, supporting elements are identified, analyzed, and prioritized by importance, need, and contribution for inclusion or exclusion into the model. Employment security as we know it today will be one such element.

Drucker predicts that the typical large business in the year 2000 will have less than half the levels of management as its counterpart of today, and no more than a third of the managers.

This relatively flat organization will require self-discipline and greater emphasis on individual responsibility for relationships and communications. Goals will have to be clearly stated, with common objectives that translate into definitive actions. Drucker perceives the new information-based organization as resembling the symphony orchestra. In the symphony, several hundred specialists play together, following the same score, and are managed by one CEO, the conductor. The specialists, the musicians, are experts focused with career aspirations within their identifiable niche of expertise. The conductor, though unable to play each instrument, can coach and coax various members to seek perfection in their specialty.[2]

The information-based organization is by no means void of challenge. Critical problems anticipated by Drucker include:

- Developing rewards, recognition, and career opportunities for specialists.
- Creating unified vision in an organization of specialists.
- Devising the management structure for an organization of task forces.
- Ensuring the supply, preparation, and testing of top management people.[3]

In projecting survival of employment security as we know it today, we must look to the future and focus on the challenges listed by Drucker, and compare them to the organization and workforce of the 21st century. This comparison will provoke discussion from which decisions can be based. The amount of "baggage" to be carried from the enterprise of the 1990's to the firm of the future need to be a major part of this discussion.

The workforce of specialists will present management challenges outlined by Drucker. The structure is projected to be flat in design with broader spans of management control, fewer levels of management in the hierarchy, and work that will be completed by teams of specialists. The evolutionary process is in motion within most major corporations in America in their quest for efficiency, focus, and survival. The challenges of creating a unified vision and management structure will need to be coordinated closely with reward systems, employee recognition, and career-path opportunities.

In this age of specialization and extensive use of knowledge workers questions remain as to whether employment security will decline or grow in numbers of subscribers. If it does survive, will firms benefit from increased company loyalty, higher productivity, and improved morale and justify this practice to their stakeholders?

Using the comparison that the organization of the 21st century will resemble the symphony orchestra, each policy and practice now offered needs to be reviewed for applicability and benefit. Change to demographics within the workforce will also play a key role in this equation.

NEW ENTRANTS TO THE WORKFORCE

The enterprise of the 21st century will continue its evolutionary process concurrently with demographic changes of new entrants to the workforce, change in job expectations, in work assigned and performed by full-time employees, and in internal operating forces and structure. Some of the changes expected for the workforce include:

1. A shortage of skilled workers is anticipated in second half of the 1990's. Workforce increased 2.7 percent in the 1970's, and will slow to 1 percent in the 1990's. There will be 26 percent fewer high school graduates entering the

labor force in 1992 than in 1977, while new jobs will be created at the rate of 1 to 2 million per year.

2. A rapid job growth in services is expected. This includes health care, finance, retail and food services. The better-paying and more challenging jobs will require education.

3. Women and immigrants will fill many of the jobs created by labor shortages. Most families will require two wages to sustain a higher standard of living. Women will represent more than 60 percent of the workforce, accounting for two-thirds of the growth in all occupations.

4. The use of part-time and temporary workers will increase and union membership (now at 17 percent of the workforce) will continue to decline. Large companies will cut middle-management jobs. Most jobs will be created in smaller companies employing 100 to 2,500 employees.[4]

The demographic change underway will affect the private and public sector. While there will be high demand for knowledge workers there is projected to be less supply than required. This shortfall of skilled knowledge workers will impact the evolutionary process.

The limited supply of new entrants into the labor force will also challenge organizational needs. According to the U.S. Census Bureau it is estimated that between 1980 and 2000 the eighteen- to twenty-four-year-olds in the U.S. population will decline by 19 percent while the overall population will increase by 18 percent. The U.S Bureau of Labor Statistics projects the mix of new entrants into the labor force between 1988 and 2000 to be different than historical numbers. Of the more than 42.8 million new entrants, only 31.6 percent will be the typical "white male."

By the year 2050 there will be approximately one worker for each social security beneficiary. The present ratio is about 3 to 1, according to the U.S. department of Health and Human Services. Based on this aging population we could suffer a shortfall of as many as 560,000 science and engineering professionals by the year 2010.[5]

The growth of jobs in the service sector, combined with increased use of part-time workers and union membership decline, will reduce some of the present emphasis and focus on employment security. Based on demographic projections the lack of skilled knowledge workers, the mix of new entrants to the workforce, the changing organization structure, and employee expectations, employment security could be a factor to entice qualified employees to public or rivate enterprises.

EMPLOYMENT SECURE ORGANIZATION OF THE 21st CENTURY

The organization structure and "employee" composition of those firms practicing employment security in the next century is evolving, and is projected to look much different than the enterprise of the 1990's. There will be fewer full-time employees. Rather than all employees receiving salary and benefits directly from the firm, employees will be comprised of a number of components. Each component will provide direct support and employment protection to "core employees."

It is estimated that core employees will contribute and directly perform approximately 60 to 80 percent of workload requirements. The remainder will be completed by the groups of workers depicted in Figure 8.1. The role of each is key to the survival and protection of employment security for the core workforce, and is described below:

Figure 8.1

**Workforce of the 21st Century
Employment Secure Organization**

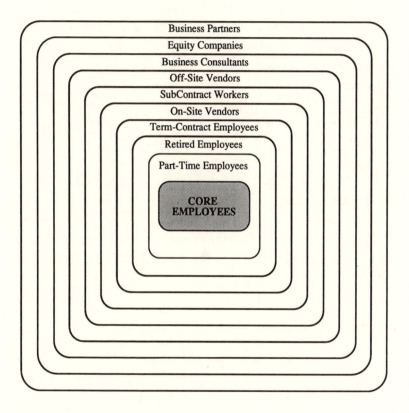

Note: Evolving Usage of Work Components in the 1990s

Core Employees

The base group of employees whose employment is protected by the firm. These employees work full-time for the company. According to Drucker, the organization now evolving will require few if any specialists in its central management structure. He says that a limited number of employees will be needed to perform central operations work such as human relations, legal counsel, or public relations. Service support staffs who provide advice, counsel, or coordination will shrink in numbers.

The remaining employees, referred to as knowledge workers, will maintain, manage, and direct the business. They will include programming, engineering, marketing, research and development, technicians, management, manufacturing, and other functions. The mix and numbers required will depend on the business need.

This group of employees may be expected to satisfy 60 to 80 percent of total workload requirements, retain basic technical knowledge of the business, and be flexible to perform work recalled from the support groups.

Business Consultant

The business consultant will be called upon to perform specific tasks such as forecasting product or market demand, financial analysis and projection, public relations, effectiveness of internal communication, or organizational analysis. The consultant role will increase in importance as companies reduce staff and middle management that perform this work in today's organization.

Part-Time Employees

Part-time or supplemental employees have been effectively used by companies since the 1940's. This group of employees fills the work gap between full-time employees and workload requirements during peak times. Part-time employees sometimes work from ten to forty hours per week, are often paid an hourly rate, receive few if any fringe benefits, and could be students, housewives, or workers supplementing another income. Jobs performed by this group range from manufacturing and basic clerical work to positions requiring professional expertise, such as programming, engineering, or marketing.

Retired Employees

In recent years a number of American companies have offered early retirement incentives in their effort to streamline staffing. These incentives have been accepted by a number of employees whose ages range from mid-forties to late sixties, and whose work experience ranges from manufacturing and clerical to executive management. The age and experience base have made attractive the reemployment of these people on a contractual or rate-per-hour agreement. This previously untapped labor source could become more utilized in the future. This segment of workers will be called upon as the labor shortage intensifies and firms require experience lost when early retirement incentives were accepted.

Equity Companies

A number of corporations underwent drastic change during the recessions of the 1980's and 1990's and reduced numbers of employees, in addition to streamlining and eliminating functional operations within their firm. There was also hesitation to venture into other business areas because of financial and other business constraints. For example, computer hardware manufacturing companies, due to limited financial resources, hesitated to enter the fast-growing area of developing, manufacturing, and marketing software products. Instead, some computer hardware companies purchased a percentage of equity in one or more software companies. This allows a firm to obtain a "lock" on a venture that it was uncomfortable about expanding directly into. Buying equity into a company provides the hardware firms with growth potential and financial support of this venture without acquiring overhead and the operational risk associated with full ownership. Investment risk was reduced through the equity venture while extending company resources into a multitude of strategically compatible enterprises. This methodology will continue to increase in usage.

Off-Site Contractor

Off-site contractors have been, and are, used for satisfying demands in manufacturing. Parts and subassemblies have been contracted for some time as a way to manage peak workloads. This use of off-site contractors in the 21st century will expand to information-based work: engineering, data processing (programming and system operations), marketing, accounting, public relations, employee training, and education.

Subcontract Workers

The use of on-site subcontract workers has also increased. Firms contract with professionals or agencies to perform needed work in functional areas such as programming, engineering, drafting, or telemarketing. This group of workers continues to show an increase in numbers in the U.S. labor force. Companies have accepted reduced commitment to full-time professionals and the associated benefits, while using this needed expertise for short-term needs. Work performed by these "employees" include contracting of services of lower-paid workers such as those required in manufacturing or clerical work, as well as those of professional knowledge workers.

Term-Contract Employees

A recent phenomenon in private companies is the advent of term-contract employees. These employees are hired to fill positions in either professional or non-professional categories. They are required to sign a contract for employment covering a specific period of time, and may or may not be provided benefits. These employees are paid to work in a specific job for a specified period of time. They often receive partial or full benefits and pay similar to that of full-time employees. Although colleges have employed this type of person for some time, as adjunct faculty, private business has not. These employees would primarily reside in companies practicing employment security to buffer workload fluctuations. Both employee and employer have commitment for the term of the contract.

On-site Vendors

The use of on-site vendors is an evolving and expanding method to have work effort completed on location by workers outside the company. For example, companies are currently hiring on-site vendors to perform facility maintenance, finance and accounting, specialized clerical work, and programming projects in addition to the more traditional vended work such as secretarial services or security. When hired, the vendor will provide onsite management and personnel to complete tasks required for that functional area. One IBM location recently announced expanded use of this outside resource and hired a company to provide on-site accounting support, facility maintenance, and secretarial and clerical support. This agreement provided IBM the opportunity to better utilize displaced management and employees for tasks more critical to the business.

In the effort to reduce overhead costs and streamline operations, companies retain knowledge workers and contract with companies to perform support role tasks such as those mentioned. This allows them to focus on the "knitting," as referred to in the Peters and Waterman book, *In Search of Excellence.*

Business Partners

Companies form agreements with supporting businesses to meet a need not otherwise satisfied. This agreement is often contractual and a non-monetary commitment to join forces. One company agrees to provide functions to another in an area in which expertise is needed. Some firms strong in engineering and manufacturing may contract with other companies for support and provision of product promotion and marketing. The companies are dependent on each other for success, and each provides expertise to the other. These relationships are bound by contracts n which expectations and measurement criteria are detailed. The financial arrangement is agreed upon, with payment made on commission with a predetermined sum of money.

Each subcontract work group provides support to core knowledge workers through completion of agreed-upon functions and provision of some level of employment protection. Some or all of the work could be "pulled back," reassigned, or increased as economic and market demands dictate. The employment-secure organization of the 21st century will require, as part of its strategy, access to and use of workload buffers such as those depicted in Figure 7.1.

WORKFORCE NEEDS

If predictions hold true, employee needs in the 21st century will require a different mix of benefits and options than is now provided. Employees will seek more flextime than today, more opportunity for telecommuting, and on-site child care. Some of these are now surfacing according to recent trends. According to Faith Wohl, director of workforce partnering at E. I. Du Pont Company, a recent poll taken by Du Pont showed that 56 percent of the males want more flexibility at work because of family concerns. This is up from 37 percent five years ago. The family concerns range from child care to parent and grandparent care.[6] Change in worker needs will be addressed for the organization of evolving knowledge workers.

EVOLUTION AND CHALLENGE

Change in corporate structure, the arrival of the knowledge worker, social and economic fluctuation, the demographic mix of entry people, and the continuing shift from manufacturing to service in the U.S. economy present challenge for the evolution underway. The Bureau of Labor Statistics estimates that by 1995, 74.3 percent of U.S. jobs will be in the service sector. Marvin Cetron, a leading futurologist and founder of Forecasting International, predicts that the percentage will rise to 88 percent by the year 2000. In defining services both sources include transportation, communications, trade, finance, real estate, and government.[7] This one transitional change in the U.S. challenges many support systems such as education, industry as we know it today, government, and the socioeconomic balance of the total system.

There are a number of other challenges that must be understood and addressed. Some have more impact than others. According to *Fortune*, some of the great forces changing management, employee expectations, and organizational structure include:

- Companies struggling to remain competitive can no longer afford to employ hives of number-crunching minions and report-writing middle managers.
- Advances in computer and communications technology are making it possible for machines to perform many traditional management chores more cheaply than people.
- Rapid growth of the service sector is attracting a fatter share of executive talent.[8]

The service-sector growth will provide challenge and opportunities. According to the Bureau of Labor Statistics projections about one-sixth of the roughly 14.5 million new jobs created in the service sector by 1995 will be executive administrative and managerial positions. This represents an increase of 22 percent from 1984. Among the fastest growing will be business services (management consulting, public relations, advertising, and lobbying) and professional services (law, accounting, and engineering).[9] This is important to recognize when addressing the remaining five-sixths of the new jobs.

The first two items listed are being addressed in corporate restructuring that is now taking place. By the end of the 1990's middle management jobs and many advisory staff positions will take their place in history, alongside the dinosaurs. Organizations, profit or non-profit, cannot afford the luxury of excess baggage in the competitive market place now present.

EMPLOYMENT SECURITY

The future of employment security will be determined by perceived and substantiated benefit that such an offering will have on the organization of knowledge workers. A number of factors will influence the outcome of this executive-level decision.

As was mentioned, the organization as we know it today is undergoing radical change from command-and-control to one with fewer levels of management and wider spans of control. Expectations from the full-time workforce will change as employees become more educated, focused, specialized, and empowered. New entrants to the workforce, their expectations, value systems, and items of importance will also be influential.

The declining role of union organizations and employee action to bargain collectively for wages, benefits and practices such as employment security will also be factors in this decision. Job availability, employee flexibility, and workforce mobility to other companies and other geographic locations will also be factors.

Ronald Krannich, author of *Careering and Recareering for the 1990's* writes that "anyone entering the job market now can expect three to five career changes and fifteen to twenty-five different jobs in a lifetime."[10] Reasons given for this job-hopping include the increase in work and family conflicts at the same time that executives show increased concern for productivity and competitiveness. "To stay competitive, people are working longer and longer hours," says Wohl of Du Pont. "But they need to reduce their hours to manage their lives."

All factors considered, management of employment security will continue both in intent and practice. The change and challenge that has been addressed will be matched with benefits to management, unions, stockholders, employees, government, and society.

SUMMARY

Employment security offers a number of positive results that are said to offset negative implications. Active practitioners proclaim advantages, discuss the struggles and challenges, and financially justify the offering to their stakeholders. Non-practitioners explicitly show their non-support through their strategies and actions.

Employee layoff is sometimes unavoidable but should be avoided at all costs because of damage incurred to employees, their families, society, and all who do business with that organization. Some continue to see employment security as a financial detriment to the organization, one with little (if any) benefit, and one that should not be pursued as America competes in the global market.

In support of the detractors, Mary Anne Devanna of Columbia University's Career Research Center points out that the costs of doing business, and therefore wages at all levels, are under increasing pressure due to global competition. "Companies now find they cannot afford to own people for a lifetime, particularly in mature and declining industries," she says. She looks more for employers to follow the model of investment banks, where compensation is "frontloaded"—offering high salaries but no promises about a lifetime career.[11]

Counter to Ms. Devanna's argument, one of the strongest proponents of employment security is Jerome M. Rosow, president, Work in America Institute, Inc., who points to constant change in the evolving organization. He says: "Employees are generally not adverse to change, but when it carries with it the threat of job loss, they will resist it, overtly or covertly. With their future secured, however, employees feel free to participate enthusiastically and even to initiate change."[12]

In this increasingly competitive world market can management afford not to offer programs to foster employee flexibility and change? The evolving organization of knowledge workers, the reduced staffs and middle managers, and socioeconomic change require employee support, flexibility, and loyalty greater than any prior organizational advancement in history.

NOTES

1. Peter F. Drucker, "The Coming of the New Organization," *Harvard Business Review*, January–February 1988, 47.

2. Ibid., 45–53.

3. Ibid., 50.

4. Julia Lawlor, "Experts: Workforce to be More Flexible," *USA Today*, 13 May 1991, 10B.

5. The Task Force on Women, Minorities, and the Handicapped in Science and Technology, "Changing America: The New Face of Science and Engineering," Interim Study, Washington, D.C., September 1988, 11.

6. Julia Lawlor, "Experts: Workforce to be More Flexible," *USA Today*, 13 May 1991, 10B.

7. Peter Nulty, "How Managers will Manage," *Fortune*, 2 February 1987, 48.

8. Ibid., 48.

9. Ibid., 49.

10. Julia Lawlor, "Experts: Workplace to be More Flexible," *USA Today*, 13 May 1991, 10B.

11. Peter Nulty, "How Managers will Manage," *Fortune*, 2 February 1987, 50.

12. Jocelyn F. Gutchess, *Employment Security in Action: Strategies That Work* (New York: Pergamon Press, 1985), ix.

Appendix I
Work in America Institute Recommendations

THE COMMITMENT TO EMPLOYMENT

1. In view of the clear net-cost advantage to employees and employer, we strongly recommend that employers guarantee that no permanent employee will be laid off or downgraded due to any labor surplus arising from internal corporate productivity/performance changes.

2. After balancing the benefits and costs of layoffs and dismissals against those of available alternatives, employers should issue the broadest commitment they can afford with respect to employment security during periods of business decline. They should also declare their intention to broaden the coverage as business success permits, creating an incentive for productivity. In addition, employers should promise that if sacrifices become necessary, they will be shared equitably across the organization.

3.   Employers should make a written commitment that, in the
      event that economic recessions make dismissals unavoid-
      able, they will actively assist dismissed employees to find
      suitable jobs with other firms.

THE NEED FOR PLANNING AHEAD

4.   Employers should institute a system of planning human
      resource needs and deployments as an integral part of the
      corporate business planning process.

5.   Primary responsibility for human resource planning should
      be fixed at the highest level of the firm, but all managers
      should be responsible for detailed human resource plans in
      their own areas.

6.   Since every significant challenge to employment security
      can be anticipated far in advance, employers should use this
      period to ensure that their responses are ready to execute at
      the appropriate time.

7.   On all matters affecting employment security, the CEO
      should regularly consult with senior-level and interna-
      tional officers of the union and invite the union as early as
      possible to join in designing and executing responsive
      measures.

LEAN MEASURES

8.   Since the accumulation of surplus employees in prosperous
      times can undermine management efforts to maintain
      employment security in hard times, employers should
      ensure that:

a. authorized workforce levels are tied to long-term workload plans;

b. employees are competent to meet the changing needs of the organizations;

c. annual operating plans can accommodate short-term increases of workload without adding protected employees;

d. production, marketing, and financial policies help to avoid sudden changes in workforce levels.

9. Every work unit in an organization should establish, by agreement with top management, tough but realistic staffing standards. If the work unit wants to add employees in excess of the standard, it should have to obtain top management permission. Adherence to standard is facilitated if:

a. all new hires are regarded as career employees;

b. all protected employees are, by agreement, willing and able to be deployed in a wide variety of assignments;

c. unsatisfactory performers are brought up to standard, reassigned, or dismissed early in their careers.

10. "Buffers"—such as overtime, transfers of people or workload, temporary employees, and subcontracting can help greatly in maintaining employment security in the face of short-term business fluctuations. At the same time, buffers may cause unwarranted side effects. Employers should, therefore, use them in accordance with clear ground rules agreed upon with employees and local and international unions.

11. Firms seeking to stabilize their workloads for the sake of employment security should focus on:

   a. stabilizing the flow of orders,

   b. maintaining growth at a sustainable rate,

   c. avoiding overdependency on a single market or customer, and

   d. achieving flexibility in the use of production personnel, plant, process, and materials.

RESPONDING TO TEMPORARY ECONOMIC DECLINES

12. As soon as employers detect the approach of a temporary decline in demand for their products or services, they should update and set in motion plans for:

   a. restrictive hiring,

   b. retrieving from temporary employees or subcontractors any work that can reasonably be done in-house,

   c. expanding the demand for output,

   d. assigning surplus employees to lower-priority work.

13. If a temporary decline in demand makes it essential to cut payroll costs faster than restrictive hiring alone can do, the company, its employees, and its unions should jointly work out arrangements for temporarily reducing either wage and salary rates or the number of paid working hours. All stakeholders in the firm should share equitably in the hardship.

14. To employees faced with layoffs, the employer should offer the alternative of remaining on the payroll and being paid the equivalent of unemployment insurance benefits while taking part in training and education programs approved by the employer.

15. Before instituting layoffs, the employer should make it clear to employees and unions that no better solution was available.

RESPONDING TO PERMANENT DECLINES OF WORKLOAD

16. Employers intent on honoring a commitment to employment security should not be deterred by the permanent decline of demand for part or all of their output. In cooperation with their employees and unions, they should make every effort to replace the lost workload, reduce costs without dismissals and, if all else fails, help dismissed employees find suitable work elsewhere.

17. In its effort to offset permanently lost demand, the employer should, after retrieving from temporary employees and contractors work that can be done in-house, consider launching new products or services, acquiring or creating subsidiaries, or accepting contracts from other firms.

18. If it becomes necessary to reduce payroll costs permanently, the employer should first try to do so without dismissals, using such methods as restrictive hiring, work sharing, phased retirement, wage reductions, and intensive productivity-raising programs.

19.   If the dismissal of protected employees becomes unavoidable, the employer should actively help them find suitable work elsewhere. The employer can provide financial bridging, pension portability, outplacement services, or retraining for those seeking new jobs; and professional and financial assistance and subcontracts for those preferring self-employment. If the area suffers from a shortage of suitable jobs, the employer should do as much as possible to create or attract replacement jobs.

ALLIANCES

20.   Employers and local and international unions in a metropolitan area or a major industrial region should band together to organize a computer-based job clearinghouse and keep it up to date. Where an area labor-management committee already exists, it should take an active part in this effort.

21.   Regional groups of employers and unions, both local and international, should form alliances to provide retraining and education for employees who have lost jobs through no fault of their own. To gain flexibility and economy, the allies should avail themselves of the services of post-secondary schools.

22.   Employers, local and international unions, and local and state governments should form alliances to diversify the job base in areas whose employment depends heavily on the fortunes of a single industry or a few firms. They should try to attract small firms that:

      a.   demonstrate potential for growth,

Appendix II
Collective Bargaining
Agreements

The following are examples of major collective bargaining agreements that have addressed employment security issues and concerns:

International Brotherhood of Teamsters/National Master Freight Agreement

Work-rule revisions, suspensions of COLA's, and no pay increases for three years in exchange for a promise not to establish non-union subsidiaries and the extension of seniority protection for laid-off workers.

Union Food and Commercial Workers/Armour, Wilson, Hormel

Wages frozen and COLA's deferred, in exchange for a promise not to close any packing house for the next eighteen months, and advance notice thereafter.

Printing Unions/Standard Gravure

Five-year moratorium on wage increases and suspension of restrictive practices, in exchange for a promise to invest in new equipment and start a profit-sharing plan.

Allied Industrial Workers/Dana–Fort Wayne Axle Plant

Labor costs to be reduced by $2 million per year, to avoid shutdown.

United Rubber Workers

Uniroyal: COLA's foregone and wages and benefits to be held below those of other major rubber companies, in exchange for comparable sacrifices by white-collar workers and executives.

Goodyear: Wage, benefit, and work-rule concessions, in exchange for agreement to build a plant in Akron and expand the Topeka facility.

Indianapolis Rubber: Pay cuts and suspension of COLA's in exchange for keeping the plant open.

United Steel Workers

McLouth: Wage cuts, suspension of COLA's, and some time off, in exchange for agreement by the company to open its books to the union.

Timken: Eleven-year moratorium on strikes in Canton plant, in exchange for a promise not to build a plant in the South.

United Auto Workers

Federal Forge: Suspension of four paid holidays and COLA's to avoid shutdown.

American Motors: Wage and benefit increases deferred for three years in exchange for a promise to keep its plant open for duration of contract, to handle all reductions in workforce through attrition (except those due to reduced sales), and give a sixty-day notice prior to outsourcing.

General Motors: Wage increases and COLA's deferred, in exchange for a promise to reopen four plants, a guaranteed income stream for high-seniority workers, lifetime guaranteed employment experiments for 80 percent of the workforce at four plants, transfer of laid-off workers, and profit sharing.

Ford Motor Company: In an agreement that set the pattern for GM–UAW, three Ford plants were designated for experiments in lifetime guaranteed employment for 80 percent of the workforce. In the Rawsonville, Michigan, plant in March 1984, employees accepted an alternative solution: the entire workforce is guaranteed at least thirty-two hours per week plus full benefits for three and a half years, in exchange for flexible assignment rights, special training programs, consolidation of skilled trades into basic trades, and establishment of work teams.

Amalgamated Clothing and Textile Workers/Xerox

Pay and COLA's frozen for one year and restrained for the next two years, less generous health insurance, work-rule changes, and abandonment of some personal holidays, absenteeism controls, in exchange for guaranteed employment for the duration of the contract.

Communication Workers of America/AT&T

A strike led to agreement on a training program for displaced workers, career development training for all workers, and income supplements for high-seniority displaced workers.

IBEW/Potomac Electric Workers

Flexible work rules, in exchange for a promise of no layoffs or pay cuts for unionized workers with twelve and one-half years of seniority.

Source: *Employment Security in a Free Economy*, 1984, 24–26.

Appendix III
Federal Legislation/
Employment Issues

Legislation	Jurisdiction	Prohibitions
National Labor Relations Act (1935)	Private Employers and Unions	Unfair representation by unions; interference with employee rights.
Civil Rights Act, Public Law 88-352 (1964)	Employers with 25 or more employees; also covers labor unions	Discrimination with respect to color, race, national origin, sex, or religion.
Equal Employment Opportunity Act (1972)	Most employers with more than 25 employees	Same as Civil Rights

Legislation	Jurisdiction	Prohibitions
Age Discrimination in Employment Act (1967)	Employers with more than 25 employees	Age discrimination in employment decisions concerning individuals between 40 and 70 years of age (revised—no upper limit)
Amended by: Executive Order 11246 (1965) and Executive Order 11375 (1966)	Federal contractors and subcontractors with contracts that exceed $50,000 and 50 plus employees	Discrimination in employment decisions with respect to color, national origin, race, religion, or sex
Vocational Rehabilitation Act (1973)	Federal agencies and government contractors	Discrimination in employment decisions against people with physical and/or mental handicaps
Vietnam-era Veterans Readjustment Act (1974)	Federal contractors and federal government	Discrimination against disabled and Vietnam-era veterans
Pregnancy Discrimination Act (1978)	Same as Civil Rights Act	Discrimination on the basis of pregnancy, childbirth, or related medical conditions in benefit administration and other employment decisions

b. are industrially diverse and have economic cycles that differ from those that prevail in the area, and

c. find a large part of their market at a safe distance from the work site.

A SUPPORTIVE ROLE FOR GOVERNMENT

23. We recommend that Congress establish a more rational balance between capital mobility and employment security, through the following actions:

a. Federal tax policy should be redefined to recognize the fundamental rights of every citizen to tax protection against economic hardship, such as unemployment. Further, tax policy should treat individuals and families with a more reasonable degree of equity as compared to corporations.

b. When employers seek favorable tax treatment in a merger, acquisition, or leveraged buyout, they should be required to show that they have provided appropriately for the security of regular employees who, through no fault of their own, have been downgraded or made surplus as a result of the transaction.

c. Employers should be allowed to take tax write-off and credits against future income (a) for expenses incurred in keeping surplus employees on the payroll during a temporary business decline, and (b) for expenses incurred in helping dismissed employees retrain for, obtain, and relocate to new jobs.

Employees dismissed without fault should be allowed tax credits against future income for (a) earnings and benefits lost between dismissal and reemployment, (b) any decrease of earnings and benefits between old and new jobs, and (c) costs incurred in retraining for, obtaining, and relocating to a new job.

d. When employers seek import protection or export subsidies, they should be required to show that they have provided appropriately for the security of regular employees who, through no fault of their own, may be downgraded or made surplus while the employers are enjoying such federal assistance.

e. Trade Adjustment Assistance (TAA) should be paid only to employees who are taking positive steps to obtain jobs in other industries (training, education, or relocation). However, the federal and state governments should counsel TAA-eligibles with regard to (a) the likelihood of exhausting benefits before being rehired, (b) the kinds of preparation needed in order to enter an occupation that is likely to remain in demand, and (c) local sources of education and training.

f. When employers submit a proposal for a major government contract, they should be required to make appropriate provision for the security of employees (other than those hired as temporaries) who are hired to perform the contract and who, at the expiration of the contract, are downgraded or made surplus through no fault of their own.

g. When employers claim accelerated depreciation of physical assets, they should be required to show that they have provided appropriately for the security of regular employees who, through no fault of their own, were downgraded or made surplus as a result of the introduction of those assets.

h. The rules of ERISA should be amended to provide that when employees are dismissed through no fault of their own, they do not lose their invested pension rights. If an employer's pension plan does not already make such provisions, employer and employee should be required to work out a mutually agreeable arrangement for the employee to retain such rights in the plan until retirement, or to transfer them into the next employer's pension plan, an IRA, or a similar deferred compensation account.

i. All employers should be required to pay a reasonable amount of severance to employees who, without fault, either are dismissed or laid off for twelve months or more. Preferably, severance pay should be service-based, at the minimum level of one week for every year of service.

24. We recommend that employers and local international unions jointly lobby for Short Time Compensation (STC) laws in those states that have not yet adopted them.

25. We recommend that employers and local and international unions jointly lobby Congress and the legislatures of STC states to make STC payable for a limited period to otherwise-eligible employees during unpaid hours:

a. for voluntary on-the-job training,

b. for remedial education,

c. for skill development or continuing education,

   d. for supplementing the partial wages of employees who
       perform work that is substantially less valuable than
       their normal work, and

   e. when they are receiving outplacement assistance.

26. The federal government should assist employers who have
     given an explicit commitment of employment security
     against business declines. The assistance should consist of
     reimbursement for the net additional costs they incur as a
     result of retaining employees instead of laying them off or
     dismissing them during a recession. This federal subsidy
     of employment security will require time and financial
     limits. However, the gross costs will be offset by savings in
     income-transfer and retraining programs, and by the con-
     tinuation of tax revenues from employed workers.

Source: *Employment Security in a Free Economy*, Work in America
Institute Study, 1984, 4–13.

Reprinted by permission of Work in America Institute, Inc.

Appendix III
Federal Legislation/
Employment Issues

Legislation	Jurisdiction	Prohibitions
National Labor Relations Act (1935)	Private Employers and Unions	Unfair representation by unions; interference with employee rights.
Civil Rights Act, Public Law 88-352 (1964)	Employers with 25 or more employees; also covers labor unions	Discrimination with respect to color, race, national origin, sex, or religion.
Equal Employment Opportunity Act (1972)	Most employers with more than 25 employees	Same as Civil Rights

Legislation	Jurisdiction	Prohibitions
Age Discrimination in Employment Act (1967)	Employers with more than 25 employees	Age discrimination in employment decisions concerning individuals between 40 and 70 years of age (revised—no upper limit)
Amended by: Executive Order 11246 (1965) and Executive Order 11375 (1966)	Federal contractors and subcontractors with contracts that exceed $50,000 and 50 plus employees	Discrimination in employment decisions with respect to color, national origin, race, religion, or sex
Vocational Rehabilitation Act (1973)	Federal agencies and government contractors	Discrimination in employment decisions against people with physical and/or mental handicaps
Vietnam-era Veterans Readjustment Act (1974)	Federal contractors and federal government	Discrimination against disabled and Vietnam-era veterans
Pregnancy Discrimination Act (1978)	Same as Civil Rights Act	Discrimination on the basis of pregnancy, childbirth, or related medical conditions in benefit administration and other employment decisions

Legislation	Jurisdiction	Prohibitions
Civil Service Reform Act (1978)	Federal government	Specifically incorporates Title VII, 1964 Civil Rights Act

Source: *Management World*, March 1985, 10.

Appendix IV
Questionnaire

The following questions were asked of Fortune 500 firms in an attempt to clarify the effects of employment security practices on employee productivity, absenteeism, length of service, and the financial performance of the firm. The questionnaire also sought demographic data and data based on the experience and expertise of human resource executives responding.

Responses were gathered and analyzed in two groups—those that practice employment security and those that do not. The first twenty-one questions sought a response (1 to 5) that ranked from definitely agree (1) to definitely disagree (5). The thirty-five questions that were asked follow:

1. The costs of an employment security practice outweigh the tangible benefits.

2. When employment security is practiced employees are more receptive to changes of job assignment.

3. Employment security cannot be justified in today's competitive environment.

4. Employee layoffs are necessary to resolve short-term workforce imbalances.

5. Companies that lay off employees are more likely to be represented by unions than those that do not lay off employees.

6. Employment security is more financially advantageous to the employer than laying off employees.

7. In my opinion, the unemployment insurance expense for my company would substantially decrease with an employment security practice.

Employment security would have a negative effect on . . .

8. company net income as a percentage of sales.

9. company net income as a percentage of assets.

10. company net income as a percentage of equity.

11. average annual sales per employee.

Do you agree with those who say employment security improves . . .

12. employee job performance.

13. employee loyalty.

14. employee job satisfaction.

15. employee productivity.

16. average employee length of service.

Do you agree with those who say employment security . . .

17. leads to employee complacency.

18. cannot be cost justified.

19. has no effect on employee attendance.

20. has no positive effect on employee morale.

21. adversely affects company productivity.

The remaining fourteen questions apply specifically to the company answering the survey.

The following four questions sought a "yes" or "no" response:

22. Some employees in my company are represented by one or more unions.

23. When/if my company closes a facility it offers to relocate displaced employees at company expense.

24. Employment security is a viable strategy for future implementation by my company.

25. My company provides a severance payment for all non–performance related separations.

The following two questions sought a prioritized ranking with "1" being top priority, "2" being second priority, etc.

26. Increases in workload in my company would be addressed by the following methods:
    a. hire additional full-time employees
    b. use subcontract personnel on location
    c. hire part-time employees
    d. work overtime hours

e. use outside vendors (off-site)

f. other (specify)

27. Reductions in workload would be addressed by the following methods:

    a. lay off employees

    b. reduce the number of on-location subcontract workers

    c. reduce the number of part-time workers

    d. reduce the use of outside vendors (off-site)

    e. control the overtime hours

    f. reduce the number of hours in the normal workweek

    g. other (please specify)

The next three questions requested company information for all statements that apply:

28. My company . . .

    a. offers employment security to all employees

    b. offers employment security to some employees

    c. offers employment security to all non-union members

    d. offers employment security to all union members

    e. does not now provide employment security

    f. has never provided employment security

    g. other (please specify)

29. My company considered/is considering employment security but questions its feasibility because:

    a. of business and economic uncertainty

    b. it does not appear to be cost justifiable

    c. it is difficult to apply to all employees

    d. the tangible benefits are not significant

    e. the intangible benefits are questionable

    f.   other human resource programs provide a better return

    g.   other (please specify)

30. My company once provided employment security but discontinued the practice due to:
    a. lost market share
    b. need to reduce short-term costs
    c. need to reduce long-term (3–5 years) costs
    d. economic fluctuations
    e. product maturity
    f. other (please specify)

The following demographic questions were asked to gather data for statistical analysis. The questions asked:

31. The average annual employee turnover rate in my company, excluding layoffs, is
    a. less than 3 percent
    b. 3 percent but less than 6 percent
    c. 6 percent but less than 9 percent
    d. 9 percent but less than 12 percent
    e. more than 12 percent.

32. The average annual absenteeism rate of employees in my company is
    a. less than 3 percent
    b. 3 percent but less than 6 percent
    c. 6 percent but less than 9 percent
    d. 9 percent but less than 12 percent
    e. more than 12 percent.

33. The average length of service of the employees in my company is
    a. less than 5 years
    b. 5 years but less than 10 years
    c. 10 years but less than 15 years
    d. 15 years but less than 20 years
    e. more than 20 years.

34. My company has been in business for
    a. less than 5 years
    b. 5 years but less than 15 years
    c. 15 years but less than 25 years
    d. 25 years but less than 35 years
    e. more than 35 years.

35. The percentage of employees in my company represented by unions is
    a. zero
    b. less than 20 percent
    c. 20 percent but less than 40 percent
    d. 40 percent but less than 60 percent
    e. more than 60 percent.

Source: Paul H. Loseby, *A Review and Evaluation of Employment Security Practices and Their Relationship to Financial and Employee Performance* (New York: Pace University, 1990), 205–208.

Selected Bibliography

BOOKS

Bell, Daniel. "The Corporation and Society in the 1970's." *Human Resources and Economic Welfare: Essays in Honor of Eli Ginzberg*. New York: Columbia University Press, 1972. 229–338

Byrne, Edmund F. *Work, Inc.* Philadelphia: Temple University Press, 1990.

Drucker, Peter F. *Managing For Results.* New York: Harper & Row Publishers, 1964.

———. *Innovation and Entrepreneurship.* New York: Harper & Row Publishers, 1985.

———. *The Frontiers of Management.* New York: Truman Talley Books, 1986.

Fein, Michael. "Motivation to Work." In *Handbook of Work, Organization and Society*, ed. Robert Dubin. Chicago: Rand-McNally, 1976.

Foulkes, Fred K. "Employment Security." *Personnel Practices in Large Non-Union Companies.* Englewood Cliffs, N.J.: Prentice-Hall, 1980.

Freeman, Richard B., and James L. Medoff. *What Do Unions Do?* New York: Basic Books, 1984.

Ginsberg, Helen. *Full Employment and Public Policy: The United States and Sweden.* Lexington, Mass.: Lexington Books/D.C. Heath & Company, 1983.

Greenhalgh, Leonard. "Organizational Decline." In S. B. Bacharach (ed.), *Research in the Sociology of Organizations* (Vol. 2, pp. 231–276). Greenwich, Conn.: JAI Press, 1983.

Gutchess, Jocelyn F. *Employment Security in Action: Strategies That Work.* New York: Pergamon Press, 1985.

Kopelman, Richard E. *Managing Productivity in Organizations.* New York: McGraw-Hill Book Company, 1986.

Loseby, Paul H. *A Review and Evaluation of Employment Security Practices and Their Relationship to Financial and Employee Performance.* New York: Pace University, 1990.

Mills, D. Quinn. *The IBM Lesson: The Profitable Art of Full Employment.* New York: Times Books, 1988.

Osterman, Paul. "Turnover, Employment Security, and the Performance of the Firm." In *Human Resources and the Management of the Firm* (pp. 275–317). Industrial Relations Research Association, University of Wisconsin, Madison, Wis., 1987.

Peters, Thomas J. *Thriving on Chaos.* New York: Harper & Row Publishers, 1988.

Peters, Thomas J., and Robert H. Waterman. *In Search of Excellence.* New York: Harper & Row Publishers, 1982.

Rosow, Jerome M., and Robert Zager. *Employment Security in a Free Economy.* New York: Pergamon Press, 1984.

———. *Training—The Competitive Edge.* San Francisco: Jossey-Bass Publishers, 1988.

Watson, Thomas J., Jr., *A Business and Its Beliefs.* New York: McGraw-Hill Book Company, 1962.

Weinberg, Edgar. *Employment Security in a Changing Workplace.* New York: Pergamon Press, 1984.

Weisberger, June. *Job Security and Public Employees.* New York: New York State School of Industrial Relations, Cornell University, 1973.

———. *Recent Developments in Job Security: Layoffs and Discipline in the Public Sector.* New York: New York State School of Industrial Relations, Cornell University, 1976.

PERIODICALS AND NEWSPAPERS

"America at Full Employment." *The Economist*, 14 May 1988, 69.

Aronowitz, Stanley. "The Myth of Full Employment." *Nation*, 8 February 1986, 135–138.

Bennett, Amanda. "Growing Small." *The Wall Street Journal*, 4 May 1987, 1.

Bennett, Amanda, and Douglas R. Sease. "Getting Lean." *The Wall Street Journal*, 22 May 1986, 1.

Berg, Eric N. "Shrinking a Staff, the Kodak Way." *The New York Times*, 4 September 1983, (3) 1.

Bernstein, Aaron. "IBM's Fancy Footwork to Sidestep Layoffs." *Business Week*, 7 July 1986, 54–55.

Blonston, Gary. "Busted Boomers: Out of Work at Mid-Life." *The Seattle Times*, 19 April 1991, A1, A4.

Bolt, James F. "Job Security: Its Time Has Come." *Harvard Business Review*, November–December 1983, 115–123.

Bortz, Jenny, Audrey Brockner, Joel Brockner, Carolyn Carter, Jeanette Davy, and Jeff Greenberg. "Layoffs, Equity Theory, and Work Performance: Further Evidence of the Impact of Survivor Guilt." *Academy of Management Journal*, 1986, Vol. 29, No. 2, 373–384.

Brandt, Richard. "Those Vanishing High-Tech Jobs." *Business Week*, 15 July 1985, 30–31.

Brody, Michael. "The 1990's." *Fortune*, 2 February 1987, 22, 24.

"Corporate Downsizing." *The Wall Street Journal*, 2 June 1987, 1.

Drucker, Peter F. "The Coming of the New Organization." *Harvard Business Review*, January-February 1988, 45–53.

"Employee Resources/Development." *People Management: A Guide For Managers*. International Business Machines Corporation; Armonk, N.Y., 1986.

Feinstein, Selwyn. "Short-Time Pay Fails To Catch On As A Way To Hold Down Layoffs." *The Wall Street Journal*, 3 February 1987, 35.

Fenton, H. Edward. "How Companies Use Productivity Measures." In Eliot S. Grossman (ed.), *Productivity: The Challenge of the 1980's* (pp. 14–30). Conference proceedings, Pace University, New York, 18 March 1983.

Foltman, Felician F. "Employment Security in a Free Economy." *Industrial and Labor Relations Review 39*, April 1986, 461–462.

Foulkes, Fred K., and Anne Whitman. "Marketing Strategies to Maintain Full Employment." *Harvard Business Review*, July–August 1985, 30–33.

Freedman, Audrey. "Reexamining Income Security: SUB vs. Guaranteed Work." *Conference Board Record*, May 1976, 20–23.

———. "Security Bargains Reconsidered: SUB Severance Pay Guaranteed Work." *The Conference Board*, 1978.

———. "The Case For A Free Labor Market." *Across The Board*, January 1985, 42–48.

———. "Perspectives on Employment." *The Conference Board*, 1986.

Gordon, George G., and Bonnie E. Goldberg. "Is There A Climate For Success?" *Management Review 66*, May 1977, 37–44.

Gorlin, Harriet, and Lawrence Schein. "Innovations in Managing Human Resources." *The Conference Board*, Conference Report 849, 1984.

Greenhalgh, Leonard. "Maintaining Organizational Effectiveness During Organizational Retrenchment." *Journal of Applied Behavioral Science*, 1982, 155–170.

———. "Managing the Job Insecurity Crisis." *Human Resource Management*, Winter 1983, 431–444.

Greenhalgh, Leonard, Anne T. Lawrence, and Robert I. Sutton. "Determinants of Workforce Reduction Strategies in Declining Organizations." *Academy of Management Review*, Spring 1988, 241–253.

Greenhalgh, Leonard, and Robert B. McKersie. "Cost Effectiveness of Alternative Strategies for Cutback Management." *Public Administration Review*, 1980, 575–584.

Greenhalgh, Leonard, Robert B. McKersie, and Roderick W. Gilkey. "Rebalancing the Workforce at IBM: A Case Study of Redeployment and Revitalization." *Organizational Dynamics*, Spring 1986, 30–47.

Greenhalgh, Leonard, and Zehava Rosenblatt. "Job Insecurity: Toward Conceptual Clarity." *Academy of Management Review*, 1984, 438–448.

Gutchess, Jocelyn F. "Employment Security Strategies." *Worklife*, Canada, 1985, 8–9.

Hansen, Gary B. "Preventing Layoffs: Developing an Effective Job Security and Economic Adjustment Program." *U.S. Department of Labor BLMR 102*, Bureau of Labor-Management Relations and Cooperative Programs, Washington, D.C., 1986.

Hershfield, David C. "Reducing Personnel Costs During Recession." *Conference Board Record*, June 1975, 20–22.

Hoerr, John. "Why Job Security is More Important Than Income Security." *Business Week*, 21 November 1983, 86.

Janeway, Eliot. "Jobs in America." *National Forum: Phi Kappa Phi Journal*, Spring 1985, 3.

Karr, Albert R. "Senate Panel Clears Bill Requiring Firms To Give Up To Six Months' Layoff Notice." *The Wall Street Journal*, 18 May 1987, 5.

Kelso, Louis O., and Patricia H. Kelso. "How Can We Achieve Lifetime Employment." *Chief Executive (U.S.)*, Autumn 1983, 29–36.

King, Albert S. "Barriers to Adopting Japanese Personnel Practices." *Advanced Management Journal*, Summer 1983, 34–41.

Kneale, Dennis. "Tough Choices." *The Wall Street Journal*, 8 April 1987, 1.

Koretz, Gene. "How Japan Inc. Profits From Low Labor Turnover." *Business Week*, 7 December 1987, 24.

———. "The Winter of Worker's Discontent." *Business Week*, 1 February 1988, 18.

Krashevski, Richard S. "What is Full Employment." *Challenge*, November–December 1986, 33-40.

Lawrence, John H. "What Kind of Responsibility Do Firms Have For Workers?" *Deseret News*, Salt Lake City, Ut., 9 September 1984, 4.

Lee, Chris. "The Argument For Employment Security." *Training*, April 1985, 8–12.

Loeb, Margaret. "Staid Delta Air Tries to Stem Losses By Following Other Carrier's Moves." *The Wall Street Journal*, 6 September 1983, 29.

Loomis, Carol J. "IBM's Big Blues: A Legend to Remake Itself." *Fortune*, 19 January 1987, 34.

Madigan, Kathleen. "Plant Closings: Why It Pays to Notify Workers in Advance." *Business Week*, 20 May 1988, 22.

Mangum, Garth L., Donald Mayall, and Kristin Nelson. "One Person's Job Security is Another's Insecurity, But Help is on the Way." *Personnel Administrator*, March 1985, 93–101.

Margolis, Nell. "DEC to bite the layoff bullet." *Computer World*, 14 January 1991.

McCarthy, Michael J. "Managers Face Dilemma With Temps." *The Wall Street Journal*, 5 April 1988, 39.

McGuire, Jean B., Alison Sungren, and Thomas Schneeweis. "Corporate Social Responsibility and Firm Financial Performance." *Academy of Management Journal*, December 1988, Vol. 31, No. 4, 854–872.

Mooney, Marta. "Let's Use Job Security as a Productivity Builder." *Personnel Administrator*, January 1984, 38.

"Morale Low Among Those Not Laid Off." *Industry Week*, 1 November 1982, 22–23.

Nelson-Horchler, Joani. "You'll Never Be Jobless Again." *Industry Week*, October 1987, 63–66.

Nulty, Peter. "How Managers Will Manage." *Fortune*, 2 February 1987, 48–50.

Nussbaum, Bruce. "The End of Corporate Loyalty." *Business Week*, 4 August 1986, 42–49.

"One American Worker in Ten Has Been With the Same Employer More Than 20 Years." *U.S. Department of Labor USDL 84-86*, Bureau of Labor Statistics, Washington, D.C., 1 March 1984.

Podursky, Michael. "Full Employment and Public Policy: The U.S. and Sweden." *Industrial and Labor Relations Review*, April 1984, 455.

Raelin, Joseph A. "Job Security for Professionals." *Personnel*, July 1987, 40–47.

Riggan, Diane. "Employment Security Revisited in the '80's." *Personnel Administrator*, December 1985, 67–74.

Roberts, Markley. "Employment Security in Action: Strategies That Work." *Industrial and Labor Relations Review 39*, July 1986, 615.

Rosow, Jerome M., and Robert Zager. "The Case For Employment Security." *Across the Board*, January 1985, 34–41.

Rubinstein, Saul. "QWL, the Union, the Specialist, and Employment Security." *Training and Development Journal*, March 1984, 81–84.

Sanders, Howard J. "Employers Tell How They Avoid Layoffs." *Chemical & Engineering News*, 3 December 1973, 13–17.

Saporito, Bill. "Cutting Costs Without Cutting People." *Fortune*, 25 May 1987, 26–32.

Schiffres, Manuel. "Challenges Future Bosses Will Face." *U.S. News and World Report*, 23 December 1985, 46.

Skinner, Wickham. "Big Hat, No Cattle: Managing Human Resources." *Harvard Business Review 59*, No. 5, 1981, 108–112.

Stevens, George E. "The Fading of Firing-at-Will." *Management World*, March 1985, 8–12.

Sullivan, Allanna. "Exxon's Sleeker Look Starting to Emerge." *The Wall Street Journal*, 2 June 1986, 6.

———. "Exxon Says 6,200 Workers are Leaving Voluntarily But Layoffs May be Needed." *The Wall Street Journal*, 5 June 1986, 10.

Summers, Clyde W. "Protecting All Employees Against Unjust Dismissal." *Harvard Business Review*, January 1980, 132–139.

Tanaka, Fujio J. "Lifetime Employment in Japan." *Review of Business*, Summer 1981, 17–21.

The Computer Revolution and the U.S. Labor Force. Committee Print Number 99-G, March 1985, prepared by Richard S. Belous for the House subcommittee on Oversight and Investigations (Bethesda, Md.: Congressional Information Service, Inc., March 1985), 28.

"U.S. International Competitiveness: Perception and Reality." *New York Stock Exchange*, Study of Trade, Industrial Change and Jobs, August 1984.

Vough, Clair F. "Productivity." *AMACOM*, New York, 1979, 39.

Weinig, Sheldon. "Guaranteed Lifetime Employment Pays Off Employee Commitment." *Management Review 73*, August 1984, 29.

Wilson, Marilyn. "What is Full Employment?" *Dun's Business Month*, February 1983, 36–39.

Zager, Robert. "Managing Guaranteed Employment." *Harvard Business Review*, May–June 1978, 103–115.

Zellner, Wendy, and Aaron Bernstein. "Smiling Fender to Fender." *Business Week*, 5 October 1987, 39.

PRESENTATIONS AND CONFERENCES

Akers, John F., IBM chairman of the board. Speech on "American Competitiveness," presented to the Detroit Economic Club, 11 February 1987.

Akers, John F., IBM chairman of the board. Speech presented at the IBM stockholder's meeting held in New Orleans, 27 April 1987.

Greenhalgh, Leonard, and T. D. Jick. "The Relationship Between Job Security and Turnover, and its Differential Effects on Employee Quality Level." Paper presented at the annual meeting of the Academy of Management, 1979, Atlanta.

Index

About the Author

PAUL H. LOSEBY has successfully managed in IBM and General Motors Corporation for more than twenty-five years. He has also managed a number of functional areas including information systems, finance, personnel, manufacturing, and production control. Dr. Loseby has taught business and management courses at the college level for more than sixteen years and holds the title of Assistant Professor.